150 YEARS OF ACHIEVEMENT 1834-1984

EILEEN L. PARSONS AND JENNIE WHEATLEY

Clever Fox®
PUBLISHING
Chennai • Bangalore

CLEVER FOX PUBLISHING
Chennai, India

Published by CLEVER FOX PUBLISHING 2026

ISBN: 978-93-7500-665-7

DEDICATION

This edition recognizes the contribution of Eileene L. Parsons to the preservation of the cultural heritage of the Virgin Islands. I thank God for her inspiration and for her drive that encourages everyone around her to strive for excellence.

Jennie N. Wheatley

ACKNOWLEDGEMENTS

The idea of "shedding light" on the achievements and abilities of those of our people who passed this way "unwept", unhonored and unsung" came as result of Government's decision to Commemorate 100 years of freedom to develop and achieve.

This booklet, though not in anyway complete, could never have been realized without the tremendous effort put forth by persons who took the time to write messages, research information — some almost forgotten — for the various sections of the "BVI Gallery of Honor" and in every way gave encouragement and advice.

It is hoped that this effort will spark an enthusiasm in the people of our Territory to come forward with information that will help in compiling a more complete record of the accomplishments of our people, our customs, and those things that make us truly unique — make us BRITISH VIRGIN ISLANDERS.

Thanks and appreciation are due to the following:

Mrs. Eileene L. Parsons
Dr. Norwell Harrigan
Ms. Enid Scatliffe
Mrs. Iris Fahie
Mrs. Eugenie Todman-Smith
Mrs. Eugenie Glasgow
Dr. & Mrs. Quincy Lettsome
Ms. Adorothy Turnbull
Mrs. Irene Hodge
Mr. & Mrs. Walter Hyman
Mr. Ivan "Skipper" Evans
Mrs. Golda Malone
Mr. Emile Smith
Mr. Owen Callwood
Mrs. Lena Blaizen
Mr. Orville Hobson
Mr. George Norman & family
Mrs. Verna Penn-Moll
Mrs. Vanita Parsons
Ms. Inez Turnbull
Mr. Elmore Stoutt
Mr. A.O. Shirley
Mrs. Jennie Wheatley
Mr. & Mrs. John Hyman
Hilda & Lincoln Hodge
Hon. Ralph T. O'Neal
Ms. Iva Varlack
Ms. Archibald Hodge
Mr. Albert Cline & Mr. Harrigan
Mr. John Dawson
Nurse Geraldine Norman
Mr. Lindy DeCastro
Ms. Janice Nibbs
Mr. Joseph Hodge
Ms. Victoria Abbott
Mrs. Eldra Benjamin
Ms. Arthur Selwood
Ms. Sandra Stout
Mr. Percy Turnbull
Ms. Adina Donovan
Ms. Carol Arneborg
Dr. Patrica Turnbull
Mrs. Rita Frett-Georges
Mrs. Judith Vanterpool
Dr. Marcia Potter
Dr. Irad Potter

Dr. Charles Wheatley for permission to use material from educational publications, including "STRAIGHT FROM US", "BO" HOG from the BVI High School.

HLSCC Staff members - Mrs. Janice Dawson and Mrs. Margarita Black for typing support, Ms. Bernadine Walters Louis and Ms. Emma Baker for editing support, Mr. Junior Daniel for Cover design.

CONTENTS

FOREWORD

Were the men who built structures like the old Methodist Church at Chapel Hill, East End, and the Anglican Church at Kingston, really ignorant?

Were the men who built sloops with mere hand tools really ignorant?

Were sailors who travelled between the British Virgin Islands and Santo Domingo without the aid of compass or any other equipment really operating by guess and by God?

Were the midwives who worked without the aid of modern equipment taking lives into their unskilled hands really ignorant?

Were the women who could sew the most beautiful dresses without the aid of a sewing machine, using needle, thread, thimble and scissors really behind the times?

Were the people who, without the aid of radio or any meteorological equipment, could sense that a hurricane was travelling not operating on some principle?

Were the people who without modern means of transportation could visit one another and care about each other's needs primitive?

Or is it a truism that the things people call stupid or ignorant are the things which they do not understand and cannot appreciate?

In an effort to try to understand our rich past to appreciate our wonderful and industrious ancestors – ancestors, skillful and ingenious, enterprising and inventive, clever and sensitive, farsighted and concerned; who toiled, sweated and even lost their lives in an effort to build these Virgin Islands – STRAIGHT FROM US looks back into our past. We talked with "walking history books", great sailors, midwives, mechanics, fishermen, grandfathers, grandmothers and great grandparents, and we are pleased to share a small part of this wealth of information with everyone.

To all the older generation who feel that students of the British Virgin Islands High School deserve to share their past experience and their knowledge, we dedicate this issue to you as our way of saying "THANK YOU".

Jennie N. Wheatley

INTRODUCTION

Lives of great men all remind us
We must make our lives sublime
And departing leave behind us
Footprints in the sand of time.

We owe much to our foundation builders. We honour our educators, our sea captains, house and boat builders, our great sportsman, our physicians, nurses, grannies and massagers, cooks and workers. These are the persons who passed on the torch which every generation must pass to the other. They passed it lit, burning brightly. May all who follow pass on a bright torch.

Jennie N. Wheatley

EXCERPTED FROM THE SEPTEMBER 1948 OF "THE TORCH", A BVI NEWSPAPER

" ... UNTIL PEOPLE WITH A GENUINE INTEREST IN THE ISLANDS AND A KEEN DESIRE TO SOLVE THE MULTIFARIOUS PROBLEMS WHICH BESET US, FILL THE SENIOR POSTS IN GOVERNMENT SERVICE, NO PROGRESS WILL BE MADE, AND UP TO THE PRESENT THERE HAVE BEEN ONLY A FEW NON-INDIGENOUS OFFICIALS WHO HAVE EVINCED SUCH AN INTEREST AND DESIRE. WE MUST, THEREFORE, SUPPORT TO THE UTTERMOST THOSE OF OUR OWN PEOPLE WHO ARE ABLE AND WILLING TO SERVE THEIR COMMUNITY."

The Torch

YOUR LIGHT SO

PUBLISHED MONTHLY
BY THE PUBLICITY PANEL
LIBRARY SERVICES COMMITTEE
BRITISH VIRGIN ISLANDS

Price 10 Cents

Government House
Road Town
Tortola, B.V.I.

It is an honour to be invited to make a short contribution to this publication which both commemorates 150 years of progress since the passing in 1834 of the Act ending slavery in British territories and looks afresh at the achievements of the people of these islands during that period.

So much has happened since 1834. Significant progress has been made across all areas of life.. The changes which have taken place in the Territory's economy since plantation dates have been well documented by Dr. Michael O'Neal. He tells of the times when conditions were such that most of the original landowners gave up working their holdings. Then, the BVI was among those poorer countries which were grouped together under the description "the other Caribbean." Now, the picture is a very different one.

Even in the short time I have lived here substantial developments have taken place, happily at a pace which is governed by a desire for advancement while preserving what is best in the traditional way of life. We have to thank many people for these achievements and it is proper that they should be remembered at this time.

New and exciting challenges lie ahead and we all take encouragement from the way in which our young people are preparing to make their own mark on the world.

British Virgin Islanders are rightly a proud people and I wish to extend my best wishes for the success of this booklet as a tribute to them and all that they have accomplished.

D. R. Barwick
Governor

Chief Minister
Administration Building
Road Town, Tortola
British Virgin Islands

Greetings on the occasion of the Commemoration of the 150th Anniversary of Emancipation. In the 150 years since the proclamation of emancipation from slavery, the people of the British Virgin Islands have applied themselves with obvious vigour to the task of building a country in which their children and children's children may live as proud, self-reliant citizens, knowing full well that true freedom cannot exist without economic security and financial independence. To this end, they have forged ahead with a great measure of political self-determination and in all aspects of economic life they are to be found playing truly vital roles.

I warmly congratulate the Co-ordinating Committee for conceiving of the idea of honouring the accomplishments of British Virgin Islanders in all aspects of life in the Territory. Indeed, in the post emancipation years our forbears fell to the task of providing an independent livelihood with dignity and enthusiasm. Let us salute today their efforts in constructing sloops that still ply our waters daily and in years past ventured all over the Caribbean. Let us salute the agricultural sloops that once traded in the U.S.V.I. Alas, today there is a very strong tendency on our part to move as far away as possible from the land and to use our hands to carve out the necessary tools for our existence.

If we are to survive in the harsh world of cut and thrust and stand tall among the citizens of the Earth, we as people must work together to free ourselves of these mental encumbrances and strive to create within the scope of our limited attributes a vibrant and productive economy.

Throughout this commemorative exercise, I would advocate that we not only look back, but that we also look to the future. The development of this Territory hinges on our combined efforts and it behoves us all to apply ourselves well. The motivating factor in all this ought to be that a secure future for the British Virgin Islands depends fully on our own initiative. Let us inspire in ourselves, as well as in our children, a respect for hard work and competence in every field, without self-depreciation, bearing in mind that it is the quality of work that we do, and the quantity of our contribution, that make our society a better place. Let us continue to strive to create and maintain a society that is a free one in the truest sense — one in which every individual may develop their own potential to the fullest.

Cyril B. Romney
Chief Minister

Deputy Chief Minister
Ministry of Social Services
O'Neal Building
Road Town, Tortola, BVI

It is a pleasure and I take great pride in adding my special uniqueness to this souvenir booklet honouring the accomplishments of British Virgin Islanders in this Territory. I feel that a booklet of this nature should be on the shelf of each household and in all libraries of these Islands.

We have come along way, but we can boast about nothing unless we look back and take stock of where we came from. We know a great deal about our history. We know where we came from. We know too, how we were brought here. We have nothing to be ashamed of. There are those who should be ashamed – not our race.

And now a bit of history regarding our development.

On the 1st August, 1834, the British Bible Foreign Society in England gave a gift (a copy of the New Testament and Book of Psalms combined in one) to every person who was emancipated and who was able to read; and also to heads of families who had children learning to read. You see along with religion, education was the supreme desideratum of the enfranchised Negroes at this time.

Schools and teachers were needed at this intermediate stage, and had the Government and Church pooled their energies to put into execution a complete and well-devised plan at the time, the majority of Negro children and young people, might have been made literate. The reasons why these people were not forthcoming as desired were:–

1. The British public and its counterpart in the Islands were against Emancipation and therefore they felt no responsibility for this; and
2. Local legislators were very reluctant to do same.

However, the Methodist Church (the main force in the region against slavery) took a firmer stand than ever before. With little help here and there from sympathetic proprietors, it continued the work in Religion and Education.

In the British Virgin Islands the catechizing and rote methods used by missionaries and their helpers were invaluable. They taught the rudiments of Religion. Listen to Isaac Watts Ten Commandments:

Thou shalt have no more Gods but me

Before no idol bow the knee
Take not the name of God in vain
Nor dare the Sabbath Day Profane
Give both thy parents honour due
Take heed that thou no murder do
Abstain from words and deeds unclean
Nor make a willful lie nor love of it
What is thy neighbour's do not covet.

Dear Readers, this intermediate stage in the life of free slaves was distinguished by the willing efforts of the Church and its people, the Methodist Church in particular. Therefore, some remarkable individual achievements were made in transplanting English trends of education and ways and means of adopting it to local needs. However, as changes came on the scene politically, economically and socially the Church could no longer carry the education load alone.

The task to put the large number of freed slaves on their feet demanded the full attention and resources of the Government. It was beyond the strength of the struggling Missionary body. Therefore, very gradually the improvement of social conditions and provisions of what we call Social Services came to be recognized as appropriate functions and obligations of Government.

Thank God today after 150 years of freedom we are quite able to stand on our feet and defend our Race. By God's continued help we will be totally free at last.

As a result of the above today we have our local British Virgin Islanders standing out in the fields of – Education, Medicine, Law, Religion and other areas. Thank God for our forefathers.

Willard Wheatley,
Minister Health Education and Welfare

Ministry of Communications and Works
Administration Building
Road Town, Tortola, BVI

One Hundred and Fifty years of freedom to develop and achieve in the British Virgin Islands is not a very long time in the evolution or transformation of societies. Yet, make no mistake about it, much has been achieved in elevating living standards through joint participation of domestic and foreign resources.

The captured African, sold into a system of forced labour was the basis of plantation economy, and history is replete with the horrors of that system which used human beings as a form of expendable capital. Its inception as well as its demise were primarily due to economic considerations. Now that it is behind us, we should look to the future accepting full responsibility for our individual fortunes.

There are two basic options that lie ahead:

1. We can follow the "Back to Africa" activists, who seek Messiahship through grievance leadership.
2. We can use political and economic freedoms to accelerate the rate of ownership and level of participation in the management of our economic resources.

The first option is the easy way out, and leads nowhere. The true path forward lies in entrepreneurial activity and the use of educational opportunities, bearing in mind that freedom is often endangered or even meaningless when it is not supported by economic strength. It therefore remains the duty of the State to ensure that the conditions for self-development and economic advancement exist; it is the responsibility of citizens to secure the fruits of freedom. If we are therefore to remain masters in our own house we should set no limitations on our abilities, thereby ensuring that "History will not repeat itself" at least, not as enslavement.

It is for me a distinct honour to contribute to this Commemorative Souvenir Booklet, and I hope that future publications will not only celebrate freedom to achieve, but also the achievement of international peace as a legacy to posterity.

E. Walwyn Brewley
Minister for Communications and Works

Long Look

Tortola, BVI

I am very grateful for this opportunity to say something about our territory and some changes since Emancipation. I would like to center my thoughts on changes that I have personally experienced – on progress.

There is much evidence of this progress – of almost incredible accomplishments – of goals realized that my grandparents never even dreamed of. I still remember quite vividly those first years. Island transportation was mainly on foot although some owned a donkey or mule, and a privileged few, a horse. To get to Road Town we walked over the hill – Hope, Bell Vue, Fort Hill – then on to town. To travel to St. Thomas, the early hours found us walking to catch a boat – the "Joan of Arc", at Baugher's Bay.

Men like Mr. Alvanley Frett and the late Claremont Davies and Richard Stoutt built the "rowling boats" as well as the bigger sloops that plied between the Virgin Islands, Puerto Rico and the islands to the southeast. Hardy sailors braved ravaging storms as they traded local produce – fish, agricultural products, charcoal, as well as handicrafts – for flour, sugar, clothes and other necessities. Many lives were affected in my village when accidents occurred at sea resulting in tragic loss of life. Those left behind had no way of knowing about these accidents until another boat could come over from St. Thomas.

Our parents sacrificed to send us to school. We had many chores to perform. There were cows to be milked and put out to pasture, provisions to be collected from the ground, water to be brought from the well – you dared not to be late or you were certain of punishment. We wore no "fancy clothes" nor carried any "nutritious snack". Walking barefoot was common as was "sugar and water and bread" for lunch. Because of distance, we didn't go home at lunchtime and, if our school outfit got wet or damaged, in most cases there was not another to change into.

We were taken to church whenever possible. We were taught to love God, to respect Him, our parents, those in authority and our neighbours. There was a sense of caring, a closeness and sharing that helped us all to accept our circumstances and be happy, even as we worked to improve ourselves.

I have said all this in order to compare "THEN" and "NOW." Today, we have made massive strides in communications. One only has to turn a knob on a radio, dial a number or switch on a television set to know what is happening anywhere in the world. The healthy art of walking is going out of style – we drive everywhere it seems. We no longer walk on mud tracks; roads have been greatly improved and paved and we own vehicles

– trucks, buses, cars, motorcycles and bicycles. Aeroplanes land and take off from our own airport and it is now common practice to eat breakfast in Tortola, have lunch in New York or supper in London.

Little sloops are no longer used to sail the seas to trade. Today we have large vessels and barges all powered by engines. Ocean going freighters call at port and cruise ships and passenger boats bring many visitors to our shores.

Our children have been moved from Church buildings to modern, well equipped schools. Our untrained teachers have been replaced by fully qualified teachers, many of whom have successfully completed degree courses. Recreational facilities have been provided and positive results are already evident. Our education program has produced professionals in various fields.

There is now a fully equipped hospital as well as district Health Clinics. Health care for the total community is greatly improved.

Politically we have progressed from a "Dependency" to a "Territory" with internal self government.

The little two-room houses of my early years have been superseded by spacious, well-equipped, beautifully designed and furnished homes. "Light" has reached dark corners where as children we thought "jumbies" lived and hillsides once covered with thorny brush are now dotted with attractive homes and gardens.

Opportunities for employment have been created. People can now stay at home and work, and many have returned from overseas. I suffered many indignities as I tried to make a living in other countries and I can sympathise with those who leave their homes and come to our shores in search of a better life.

Yes! We have prospered! We own many things: houses and lands; cars and boats; and – money. We have made significant progress, politically, economically, financially, educationally and in our health services. I must sadly note, however, that in our march forward, we have dropped by the way many of the values that contributed to our survival. As we celebrate our FREEDOM and PROGRESS let us return to the moral code that we knew. Let us be honest and caring citizens; let us once again respect the "Home" as the unit, and let us remember that "Except the Lord builds the house they labor in vain that build it; except the Lord keeps the city, the watchman waketh but in vain." May we NEVER abuse the Freedom purchased at a cost, nor BECOME SLAVES to money, greed, lust or power.

Terrance Lettsome
Member Opposition

Department of Education and Culture

Road Town, Tortola, BVI

It is a pleasure to participate in this magazine to mark the 150th year of Emancipation after the abolition of slavery. Here in the British Virgin Islands we are privileged to have the freedom to do almost anything we desire, and we are free from many of the problems that face some of the more populated countries of the world. Many of us cannot truly understand hunger, because we live in a land where there is plenty to eat. Our freedom also allows us to experiment, invent, change and implement new technologies as society advances and we should endeavor to direct these activities to the improvement of the qualities of life in our Territory. This legacy of freedom has been given to us for this purpose.

Unfortunately, all of us as British Virgin Islanders, as leaders, as educators, as Christians, as workers, as entrepreneurs, or as statesmen cannot claim that we have always served our country faithfully; that we have always loved our fellowmen, sought to uplift them and used our freedom to build national pride and enhance the civic mindedness of our people. We are still plagued with greed and selfishness, individual aggrandisement, low esteem for things of national interest, and more concern for self than for country.

Perhaps if 1984 is to be really meaningful to us we should address the question of our destiny as a "nation", try to decide on some national goals and begin to chart our course to achieve these goals. Our youths need to know where we are sailing to in this fourth quarter of the Twentieth Century. I appeal to all those in authority to take their leadership responsibilities very seriously and guide us in this process of nation building.

I do not intend to turn this theme of happiness, merriment and rejoicing into "sour cream". We should by all means rejoice in the victories won and progress we have made and to this end I wish everyone joy and happiness throughout 1984. In wishing you that happiness, also appeal to you to let your actions bring respect and dignity to quality of life in these lovely islands. DO NOT RAPE THE VIRGINS!

Charles H. Wheatley
Chief Education Officer

PROUD SENIORS GRADUATED FROM A COMPUTER PROGRAMME— 2001

WITH EMANCIPATION COMES EDUCATION

One hundred and fifty years have passed
From Emancipation to Education at last
From writing on clay and dirt strewn floors
To computers, calculators and shuttles with claws
The African man has done well we say,
From a slave to a spaceman flying away
No more does MASSA write and tell him his name,
Nor tell him that two plus two and four are the same
For he has walked the path of education and fame
Nor more ignorance and slavery again.

Class V. 2
Althea Scatliffie Primary School

Education Week Booklet 1984

B V I

Gallery

of

Honour

Our Educators

"On Monday morning, bright and early
Not tired, vexed or even surly,
One rose to tread the path "over the hill"
Without a whimper, but with a will,
To arrive in time for school
For this was the best and safest rule."

"The Good Old Days" *by Pearl Smith* – STRAIGHT FROM US – VOL I

In the old days a rivalry existed between the children who attended the Road Town schools. It was often a case of "Town" children against the "Country" children cannot be ascertained, but the Anglican school children delighted in calling the Methodist School Children "chapel pigs". This taunt was returned with the Methodist Children shouting "church hogs".

The story is told of the day when a group of Anglican children came up the street to taunt and torment the Methodist children, and had to pass the old "Fireproof" where there was a large hive of bees. The bees were aroused and started swarming with some settling in the hair of the Anglican child. A teacher responded to this crisis with the admonition that Anglican children would take this a warning and stop saying "chapel pigs" thereafter.

Children who attended the Anglican school a long time ago would have been taught by the following either as head teachers or as class teachers.

Charles Simon	Ruth Amey
Vitalita Dawson	Gladys Simon
Leona O'Neil-Harney	Olva Flax
Angelica Scatliffé	Francis Filbert
Isa Roberts	Rev. John Haddock
Mr. Semper	

Rev. John Haddock taught in Virgin Gorda and was father of Miss Belle Haddock, whose home is still across from the Cable & Wireless building in Road Town.

Mr. Semper – first name unremembered – was from St. Kitts. He built the first school in the Valley, Virgin Gorda.

Mr. Simon's name cannot be separated from St. George's Anglican School. He was an Antiguan who headed that school for many years and turned out many outstanding scholars.

In the decades of the 1920's and 1930's almost every head teacher came from one of the Leeward Islands. Very little attempt was made to train the locals, no matter how brilliant they appeared to be.

Head teachers and class teachers of the Methodist Schools:

Samuel Harrigan
Beatrice Buckley
Stanley Nibbs
Reubena Brewley-Connor
May Lloyd-Smith
Viola Norman
Cecil Edwards
Juliette Georges-Fahie
Gladys Hodge-Wattley
Florence Thomas
Jonathan Richards
Hilda Christian
Harold Roberts
Enid Scatliffé
Lincoln Hodge
Loubelle Penn-Heywood
J.E.T. Roberts
Charles S. Elmes
Ann Alicia Forbes
Norwell Harrigan
Isabella Morris
Breggatto Flax
Thomas E. Ryan
Azelia Milliner
Millicent Henley-Christopher
Charles Greenaway
Stanley Smith
Stanley Gordon
Irma Dawson Gordon
Raymond Penn
Gwendolyn Smith Rhymer
Lyra Smith Liburd
Valaria Malone Wheatley
Leonora Melville
C. Howard Greenaway
Ivy Adams Creque
Eva Wheatley Davies
Rosalind Davis Varlack
Una Davies Penn
Gloria Turnbull-Hill
Adeline Creque Leonard
Willard Wheatley
Althea Scatliffé
Vera Shirley
Claudia Vanterpool-McGill
Leoteal Hodge
Rose Davies Carrot
Hershal Smith
R.D. Beamish
Maurice Henry
Lucia Potter Walters
Alexandrina Maduro
Lillian Simon
Louis Walters
Dagmar Scatliffé Hodge
Sylvia Smith
Adorethy Turnbull
Inez Turnbull

Samuel Harrigan, grandfather to Dr. Norwell Harrigan, was not only a school teacher, but was also a local preacher.

Lincoln Hodge was headmaster at both West End and Jost Van Dyke, then worked at the Treasury when he completed his service.

Juliette Georges-Fahie went on to teach in St. Thomas in the public schools where she worked until the time of her death.

Miss Ruby (Reubena Brewley-Connor) loved music and was one of the first persons to be crowned "Calypso Queen" during the August Festival. Her rendition of "Gin and Coconut Water" electrified an August Festival Village audience, thus winning her the coveted crown.

What Mr. Simon did for the Anglican School, Miss Beatrice Buckley did for the Road Town Methodist School. She held the reins there from the mid-20's up to the mid 30's ably supported by Miss Althea Scatliffé. Miss Buckley relocated to St. Thomas where she operated a dry-goods store for many years.

R.D. Beamish and Loubelle Penn-Heywood gave instruction to the first group of British Virgin Islanders to enter the "Secondary School" – "a new innovation" in education for the British Virgin Islands in 1943.

Maurice Henry an Antiguan headed the East End Methodist School in 1949 while Willard Wheatley received training in Trinidad.

MISS ALTHEA SCATLIFFÉ REMINISCES

I was born in 1894 at HENLEY'S – an area on the road to Brewers Bay, Tortola. At the age of nine I attended school, which was then housed in the Road Town Methodist Church Hall. Children from Cane Garden Bay, Carrot Bay, Brewers Bay and the country districts attended the same school.

I was above average ability since I was fortunate to have a mother who owned a private school, and was able to teach me during my pre-school days. My mother lost her life in a hurricane in 1916.

I can still remember an incident that took place when I was in Seventh Standard. Every year the Inspector (the Inspector came from overseas) would come to the School to hold examinations. The Headteacher made a list showing what students achieved in the different subjects, and gave the Inspector. We had to be in our seats when the Inspector arrived or we would have it for that day.

This particular day another student and I went out at lunchtime to look for genips from a large tree not too far away. We were so busy getting our genips that we did not hear the bell. Somehow we happened to see the Inspector going through the gate. We forgot about the genips and took to our heels. We went through another door at the back and were in our seats just as the Inspector entered the front door. You can imagine how breathless we were at this time, but trying hard not to show it.

Believe you me, if we had been asked a question at that time, we couldn't possibly have answered. If we had not been in our seats punishment would have been worse. I was in Seventh Standard (the highest grade) and there were but a few in this class.

My teaching career began in 1910 and ended in 1954 when I retired. I taught in Road Town and Anegada. Shortly after I began teaching, I became ill and was away for about a year and a half. I spent about 5 years 3 months in Anegada. The roll at that time was between 50 and 59. I was always hoping that it would reach 60, but it never did.

In those days it took a boat five or six hours from Road Town to Anegada, but if the breeze was from the North it might even take longer, as the boat was often blown backwards. The sailors left Road Town around 11:00 p.m. or 5:00 a.m. to get to Anegada while there was still daylight. When the boat reached a certain distance off Anegada (there were no wharves) a man in a flat bottom boat would come out to get the people. Sometimes you were taken across in somebody's arms; and if that somebody had something against you, he was apt to " stumble."...

English was a subject I liked very much and more classes were held in this subject than in any other subject. So much so, that my scholars claimed that I gave them too much English. One student, now Dr. Norwell Harrigan, even commented that English gave him indigestion but he was glad that he did swallow it.

I came out of retirement recently and opened a private school, after being asked by more than one parent about teaching their children. Today I have a private school attended by three and four year olds.

From "Miss Althea Scatliffé Reminisces" by Miss Althea Scatliffé. Copied from "STRAIGHT FROM US", Vol. 1 No. 2 published by BVI High School

**

Miss Althea Scatliffé (second row, third from left) and some of her students ranging from Pre-Primary to Chief Education Officer (second row-fourth from left)

**

BVI High School students attempt to relive some features of past life in the B.V.I.

Excerpts from "THE INSPECTOR'S VISIT" by Mr. Stanley Nibbs

From 1872 to 1956 the British Virgin Islands were a presidency of the Leeward Islands with the Governor residing in Antigua. Education was also administered from Antigua until 1940. During that time an annual inspection of schools was made. The Inspector came from Antigua to inspect the schools and test the progress of education. Indeed, this was quite an occasion.

For many months before his arrival great preparations were made. Every subject, namely – Reading, Writing Arithmetic (mental and written) Recitations, Geography, History, Elementary Science, Moral Instruction and English was learned by rote to present proudly in order that the school and its teachers would gain prestige.

The parents and pupils also worked hard to purchase the necessary clothing and materials, and on the appointed day every boy and girl, rich and poor, came dressed in their best. Many wore shoes that were stuffed; while others limped in pinching ones. Late comers were encouraged to make a special effort, and it was a pleasure to see the 10 and 11 o'clock pupils trooping in at 8:30 a.m.

On the morning of the examination you can only imagine the suspense with which we awaited his arrival. We sat at our classes as still as mice but with hearts pounding. On the Inspector's arrival, all attired in white and accompanied by the Methodist Minister, we were relieved as we stood at attention and lustily sang the British National Anthem. After this he was welcomed and introduced by the Minister, and the inspection began.

The classes were at first all inspected generally for cleanliness and general arrangements. The classes comprised Juniors A & B, Lower Division consisting of Standards 1 and 2, Middle Division which comprised Standards 3 and 4, and the Upper Division which included 5, 6, and 7. The subjects examined in the Juniors were Writing, Reading, Tables and Mental Arithmetic.

In the Lower Division – Reading, Writing, Arithmetic (oral and written) Moral Instruction. Written work in Arithmetic in this Division was set on little cards (blue, green, red and yellow in color) and we felt like college students when we received our examination cards. The examinations in the Lower Division were completed by 12:00 and the lower forms were given a half day holiday. In the Middle Division the subjects examined were the three R's and West Indian Geography.

In the Upper Division the subjects taken were Arithmetic, Geography, English, History, Elementary Science, Anatomy, Hygiene, English Language and English Grammar (analysis and parsing). I well remember the Inspector, Mr. James giving this sentence to Standard VII for oral analysis:

"Teach me to live that I may dread
The grave as little as my bed."

In the Upper Division the examination took the morning and evening sessions, generally ending between 3:30 – 4:00 p.m. The climax came when the reports of the examinations were received and read out. It was a time of rejoicing and especially so if the pupils had acquitted themselves well; the school received a good recommendation and the largest number of passes. That school was then considered the best in the British Virgin Islands.

EDUCATION IN THE BRITISH VIRGIN ISLANDS–The First Hundred Years

1835 The first allocation of the **£200** due to the British Virgin Islands from the Negro Educational Grant – to be administered by the churches – was made. The islands registered 5,792 emancipated slaves; four Anglican schools – two in Road Town, one at Kingstown, and one in Virgin Gorda. The Methodist School in Road Town had a much larger enrollment than its Anglican rivals in Road Town.

1837 Hurricane destroyed the Methodist school buildings at East End and West End. There was a suspension of educational activity at Jost Van Dykes due to shortage of funds and at Kingstown where the school building was converted to a refuge for hurricane victims. The Anglicans established a school at Anegada but due to lack of funds this and a similar effort at Salt Island were discontinued.

1844 The Virgin Islands Endowed School for Boys, a grammar school financed by students' fees and registering 17 pupils was opened.

1859 The Legislature was forced to appropriate an ordinance in the sum of £50 per year and appoint a supervisory Commission to ensure the reorganization of schools.

1864 There were on the islands nine schools serving about 600 children.

1882 A Commission inspection report recorded "an unfortunate state of education."

1898 Compulsory education for all children from ages five to twelve living within two miles of an elementary school was enforced.

(Excerpted from "The First Hundred Years" by Pat Turnbull for Education Week 1984)

A TRIBUTE TO MISS AGUSTA FORBES

Of Sea Cow's Bay Who After Emancipation Made The First Step In The Education Ladder To Freedom In That Area. (By children of Ebenezer Thomas Primary School)

Twas in the cool she started her school
Under the mango and tamarind tree
She started with five, and they ran to hide
As people were passing by.

She taught them to read, she taught them to write
She taught them to like the things that were right
A faithful few brought her a happens
While all the others ate their school fee

As time went by the boys cut down sticks
And wattled a shed right over their heads
Others brought palm leaves, dry grass and with
To thatch a shelter to keep out the weather

After the children wrote, ciphered and read so well
The church acknowledged her effort and threw open their doors
She took her easel, slates, board, strap and bell
And there's no telling how the news spread.

She attracted children from Sea Cows Bay,
Doty, Chalwell and Meyers
Todman, Diamond and Harrigan for years
Her classes grew from Infants to Class Two
And fed the Road Town Schools right through

A stricter and kinder person you couldn't find
She always insisted on your being on time
She rolled those R's, sounded her T's and D's
And made you mind your Q's and P's

One cannot forget the atmosphere she created
Of tolerance, mutual respect and understanding
These have already germinated
And the trees of her garden
With seeds dispersed in many isles
Have long been established

Ours is a humble tribute
For a job well done
As we salute a great teacher
MISS AGUSTA FORBES

A BENEVOLENT LETTER – A gift from the Nottinghams

We set off through a dense thicket to Long Look, the ancient home of Samuel and Mary Nottingham, (Friends of Bristol, England). About sixty years ago these enlightened and benevolent Friends, who owned and occupied this estate, returned to England after having manumitted their slaves, and made them a deed for the property as a compensation for their services. They also furnished them with a letter of advice suited to their new condition, which we were glad to discover had been successfully attended to. This letter is considered by the present occupants as one of their choicest treasures, and was handed to us soon after our arrival at the house of Jasper Rabsat, one of the oldest members of this little community. The following is a copy:

Bristol

30th of Ninth month, 1782

Dear George,

Thy letter of the 8th of Sixth month last was received, which was very pleasing to us to hear of the present good disposition of thyself and the rest of our late servants, whose welfare and happiness, both here and hereafter, we have much at heart. But we are sorry to hear of the removal of poor John Venture, and Harry, though we are not without hope of their partaking of that mercy which is extended to all without respect of persons, whether white or black.

So George, remember what we write to thee, we write to all of you who once called us master and mistress. But now you are all free, as far as it is in our power to make you, because none are free indeed, except they are free in Christ. Therefore we admonish you, not as your master and mistress, but as your friends and benefactors, beseeching you to be cautious of your conduct, and circumspect in your behaviour to all, that none may accuse you of abusing that freedom, which we in the course of divine Providence have been 8able to give you. Remembering also, that as free men and women, ye stand accountable for every act of your conduct, and must answer for the same in your own persons, if ye do amiss. In which case the laws where you are, have provided a punishment according to the nature of the offence. But do well, and ye shall have praise of the same. And that you may be able to live honestly among men, we have given you our East End plantation on Fat-Hog Bay, with every thing thereunto belonging, which we will endeavour to have secured to you by all lawful ways an9d means, that none may deprive you or your offspring of it, but that you may freely cultivate and improve it to your own benefit and advantage, and thereby b10e provided with a sufficient subsistence to live comfortably together, in all friendliness and cordiality, assisting each other, that those more advanced in years may advise the younger, and these submitting to the counsel of the elder, so that good order and harmony may be preserved among you, which will assuredly draw down the blessing of the M11ost High.

Mary and Samuel Nottingham

The meeting arrival of Mr. Thomas Dixon Green, B.A. Oxford University. Taken from the September and October 1942 issues of the "VIRGIN ISLANDS OFFICIAL BULLETIN". Excerpts from the writing of Dr. Wailing in the September issue and from the writings of Mr. C.S. Elmes in the October issue.

...On August 26, 1941, as Commissioner, attended a food control conference in St. Thomas. While in St. Thomas I had the pleasure of meeting Mr. Green and brought him back to Tortola with me. Mr. Thomas Dixon Green, B.A. of Oxford University, has been appointed Headmaster of the proposed Government School to be built in Road Town, and upon his arrival took charge of Education, relieving Reverend Davison who has been assisting the Government in the capacity of Supervisor of Education. I take this opportunity to of thanking Mr. Davison for his assistance. Mr. Green has been studying West Indian Educational problems in St. Vincent since early May and has also spent five weeks in Trinidad. On his way here he spend a week in St. Thomas getting acquainted with the educational authorities there. This, last and the fact that Mr. Green has studied most of the literature on the Virgin Islands and is already exceptionally well informed which displays enthusiasm and interest.

I am confident that with a young and energetic leader, specifically engaged for the purpose, Education enters upon a new era, if—you cooperate. Mr. Green comes with a reputation as a sportsman, and if he can impart this quality to our peoples, his efforts will not be in vain. He has great opportunities, and I trust he will make the most of them. I am sure he will have the good wishes of all who get to know him.

Thomas Dixon Green

14th February 1918 – 18th July 2012

St Oswald's Church

Fulford, York

THE COMMUNITY WELCOMES THE NEW EDUCATIONAL LEADER - C.S. Elmes

On the evening of September 4 a homely gathering, constituting a representative section of the community met in the Anglican schoolroom at Road Town to welcome Mr. Green as Supervisor of Education and Headmaster of the proposed Government School.

The meeting was opened by Mr. C.S. Elmes, President of the Teachers Association, who after stating its objects and commenting briefly on its significance from the educational standpoint, announced His Honour, Dr. D.P. Wailling as Chairman.

In a terse and impressive manner His Honour welcomed the new officer on behalf of the Government and community; informed him of his duties, and wished him a happy term of service in these islands.

Speaking for the community at large Mr. Howard Penn, a prominent citizen and a member of the Board of Education, gave an address in which he outlined in bold, yet unmistakable terms, what he considered to be the educational needs of the people. It is true to say that the thorough way in which Mr. Penn dealt with his subject should have left no misapprehension in the mind of the new supervisor as to the nature of the task with which he was faced.

The Reverend Father Wilson of St. George's was next to address the audience. In his usually attractive manner this Reverend gentleman pleaded with all sections of the community—from important Government officials and school managers to ordinary children going to school—to give the new officer their whole-hearted support; he laboured to convince his hearers of the need for cooperation with their new leader in every respect so as to make work effective and useful.

Mr. Norwell Harrigan spoke on behalf of the teachers. In an enthusiastic speech he pledged the full and willing support of the Teachers Association to the new educational chief and stressed among other things the need for the establishment of such mutual relationships between employers and employees as would enable them to meet on common ground to discuss problems of common interest.

At this point the meeting the Chairman called on Reverend Davison of the Methodist Church to introduce Mr. Green to the audience. It was then that the meeting learned to its great satisfaction that their young and energetic leader was a brilliant student who was fully qualified to discharge the duties assigned to him. The speaker said that Mr. Green was educated at Oxford University where he obtained First Class Honours in Modern History and took the Teachers Diploma in Education while his six months of observation in the Windward Islands had given him practical knowledge of the West Indian system of education.

It was now Mr. Green's turn to reply to the various speeches in which reference had been made to him and his new appointment and needless to say everyone was anxiously waiting to hear the unaccustomed voice of the man who formed the nucleus of attention for the evening. In language that was as simple as the tone in which it was delivered was pleasing, and with a poise that denoted humility rather than exaltation, the new officer expressed his pleasure at being in his new sphere; graciously thanked those who were responsible for the very fine welcome that had been extended to him; and implored the cooperation of all in the work which lay before him. With the wisdom becoming an officer in his position, he refrained from making any rash promises which as yet he could have no hopes fulfilling, but assured his hearers he would do all in his power for the good of education in this Presidency.

The meeting was brought to a close by Mr. Philbert, Secretary of the Teachers Association who in fitting terms thanked all who had taken part in making the evening a success. So ended a meeting of great significance. It provided an opportunity for bringing Government policy before the public so that it might be better appreciated. The people of the Virgin Islands moreover, had confidence and good will towards their new educational leader and he in turn had accepted the cordial welcome and pledged the full benefit of his service to their educational advancement. In the establishment of this first contact between the Supervisor and the people he has come to serve, it is to be hoped that there has been sown on good ground a good seed which will in due time grow and bring forth abundant fruit.

C.S. Elmes
B.V.I, Teachers Association

FROM THE APRIL, 1943, ISSUE OF THE VARGIN ISLANDS OFFICIAL BULLETIN EDUCATION

A PLEA FOR BVI SCHOLARSHIP TO ANTIGUA GRAMMAR SCHOOL

During January this year, an event of great historical importance to the British Virgin Islands took place. This event was the arrival of Dr. Reginald H. Georges, a native of Tortola to be Junior Medical Officer of the BVI for a short period.

Such an event had not occurred for over a century, when John Lettsome, a native of Jost Van Dyke, BVI returned to the Virgin Islands to practice medicine in the British Virgin Islands, being the same Dr. Lettsome who later achieved medical prominence in England (became physician to the King—Ed.) and was also the writer of the familiar lines:—

"I John Lettsome Blisters, bleeds and sweats 'em' If after any choose to die I, John – lets 'em."

The arrival of Dr. Reginald Georges as a Medical Officer marked an important milestone in the history of the BVI, for whereas Dr. Lettsome, though born in the BVI, his success cannot fail to be an inspiration to all native Virgin Islanders and a credit to his entire family and race, now that he has gone to Antigua to be married and to practice medicine there for some time we of the Virgin Islands extend to him our sincerest wishes for his continued success in all endeavours and for happiness in married life.

But further success of Dr. Georges will undoubtedly stir the ambition of many a native and make some think of attaining to much more than the narrow confines of the Virgin Islands permit. Dr. Georges has been able to become qualified in his profession because among other factors, fortunately his parents were able, and had foresight enough to give him a chance. Probably many another boy in this Presidency would make good if proper chances were afforded. Lack of financial ability has always been one of the greatest obstacles to most endeavours here, but in a world that is constantly proclaiming that one of the great aims for mankind is "FREEDOM FROM WANT"; the iron chain of penury cannot be permitted to keep an entire people from achieving their natural progress, therefore in keeping with the present constructive spirit of making needed services available to those who otherwise could not obtain them, I suggest that a free scholarship, fully paid for from the British Virgin Islands, be established to the Antigua Grammar School to put such student in line for competing for the Leeward Island Scholarship to some University where professional studies can be undertaken.

Some provision should be at the same time made that any such student who qualifies, should be expected to render some specific period of service here, or within the Colony. The existence of the scholarship would be a great asset to the Presidency and would encourage their children in school to make greater efforts and sacrifices in the hope of winning the scholarship and the reward that would naturally follow success.

SENIOR SCHOOL

It is hoped to make a provisional opening of the Junior Secondary School in Road Town at the beginning of the Summer Term, on May 3, 1943. War conditions and especially the scarcity of lumber, have inevitably reduced the scope of the school, but I believe that, even so, it will meet a real educational need for the children of the elementary schools.

The school will be held in temporary quarters; the three large rooms of the house in which I am living in Road Town will be used as classrooms. We are hoping to start with about 40 children. No fees will be charged and the school is open to all suitable children in the British Virgin Islands, I have been encouraged by the response of parents in the country districts of Tortola and out-islands who are ready to make sacrifices in order that their children may come to this school.

The school day will begin with morning prayers and notices, and then the children will divide into forms by sex for school work. Mr. N. Harrigan will teach Agriculture, Elementary Science, and Mathematics. Miss L. Penn will take the girls in Cookery, Needlework, Housecraft and Hygiene. I shall be in charge of the Arts Subjects – English, Geography and History. It will not be possible to find full-time employment for Mr. M. Donovan, for there is no lumber for which to have woodwork classes, but he will teach Geography, Drawing (freehand and mechanical) and Geography (especially mapping) for two full days in the week. Games will be played on Friday afternoons. The details of syllabi and the time table remain to be worked out, and at first they must be very elastic.

The obstacles which must be overcome are many, and they can only be met successfully with the cooperation of all. The school is going to cost more to run than the Elementary Schools, and therefore, a high standard of achievement will be expected. Membership of the senior school must be a coveted privilege, and the chosen children must realize that they are expected to come to school each day of the week and that the school begins promptly at 9:00 a.m. We shall have no option but to send defaulters back to the elementary schools. Parents of selected children will receive individual notification of the opening of the school within the next fortnight.

We have all waited long for this school. I shall do all that I am able to ensure it a success; the rest is up to you.

T.D. Green
Supervisor

SLOGANS

A Little Tid-Bit from the September, 1942 issue of the BVI OFFICIAL BULLETIN

On Wednesday 12th August the U.S. Coastguard cutter arrived from St. Thomas with Mrs. Ernest Hemingway. Mrs. Hemingway is the well-known author whose best known book is "For Whom the Bell Tolls." She herself writes for COLLIERS Magazine under her maiden name of Martha Gellhorn and has travelled widely across Europe for her writing, having spent time in Spain during the revolution. She has come out for material for an article on the West Indies and visited Road Town in quest of a sloop to take her through the

Leeward Islands landing eventually in Antigua, after visiting Virgin Gorda, Anegada, Anguilla, St. Martin, Saba, St. Kitts, Nevis and others. Needless to say the men tried to dissuade her from this venture; a long trip alone in a small sloop, with little suitable accommodations; and in the worst month of the hurricane season.

To her these must have seemed small matters in comparison with the hazards of a Spanish Civil War, and Mrs. Hemingway was not to be deterred, so we strolled down to Town to see what arrangements could be made. Within an incredibly short space of time, and most appropriately, Sloop "PILOT" had been selected.

Consequently when the Cutter left for St. Thomas at 4 p.m. Mrs. Hemingway was left behind, busily engaged in preparations for an early start next morning. Thursday morning broke rainy....It rained in torrents most of that day, but the following day broke fine and when we looked out, "PILOT" was not in the harbour; the adventure had started. We wish Mrs. Hemingway a safe voyage and a worthwhile article, although I imagine the trip alone would provide an interesting enough story.

Some of the SLOGANS submitted to commemorate 150 years after Emancipation.

Slogan	Submitted by
"Unbound in '84 boundless in '84"	David O'Neal
"August Monday did it; Today the sky's the limit"	Leona Harney
"Opportunities galore; since 1834"	A. Maduro School
"Light Freedom's path with industry And let's press on past one-fifty"	Mrs. Pat Turnbull
"Gone are the lashes, chains and bars Now we journey to the stars"	Mrs. Leona Harney
"Come, have fun! 150 years since Massa day done!"	Mrs. Maureen Welsh

COVER OF THE BRITISH VIRGIN ISLANDS
OFFICIAL BULLETIN JULY, 1942

COVER OF THE BRITISH VIRGIN ISLANDS OFFICIAL BULLETIN JULY, 1942

BRAVE BVI SEA CAPTAINS, BOAT BUILDERS AND BOATS

"They that go down to the sea in ships that, do business in great waters; these see the works of the Lord, and his wonders in the deep." Psalms 107:23

BRAVE

BVI SEA

CAPTAINS

BOAT

BUILDERS

AND

BOATS

"Our wives and children we commend to Thee
For them we plough the land and plough the deep"...
So "Pull for the shore, sailor pull for the shore
Heed not the rolling waves, but bend to the oar."

Men who helped to build a great future on the seas of the British Virgin Islands.

(Image of a man) Mr. Ernest Pickering, a sea captain for many years

Old and new merge at Baughers Bay - The Empress of Tortola in the foreground In the background masts of C.S.Y. Yachts

Mr. Watson White

(Image of a man working on a boat frame) Mr. Watson White

Watson White spent many years in boat building in Anegada. Geoffrey Brooks, an American and lecturer at H. Lavity Stoutt Community College (HLSCC), caught the flame and continues to keep the interest in the Tortola boat alive. The book Tortola Boat by Edwin Doran should be reprinted and preserved so that future boat builders can appreciate one of the great Virgin Islands legacies.

Shipwright Mr. Edwe Hodge of Towers, West End

Mr. Benjamin Albert Romney of Towers, West End

Mr. John Hodge of Frenchman's Cay ("Brother John")

Mr. Fritz Penn of East End at 97 Still going strong while he knits a turtle net

LAUNCHING OF 'RESPECT' BUILT BY EDWE HODGE,
OWNED BY WILLIAM RHYMER

LIST OF CAPTAINS AND SAILORS

The Captains and sailors of the British Virgin Islands were once regarded as the most ingenious sailors of the sea. The Captains and owners of the sea-worthy British Virgin Islands crafts together with their sailors journeyed to many islands of the Caribbean such as the U.S. Virgin Islands, Puerto Rico, Santo Domingo, Anguilla; some even ventured as far as Trinidad. Our gallery of honour, though in no way complete begins below:

EAST END/LONG LOOK/MAJOR BAY	
Milford Chalilwell	OCTAVIA C
Dennis Potter	SANTA LU/SEA FOX
Joseph Smith	DAISY/LADY SMITH
Reginald Thomau	PERSEVERANCE
Milton Thomas	THE RUBY
James Thomas "Bim"	TRIUMPH
Ellis Rabsatt	KING FISHER
Alexander Lettsome	RALEIGH
Charles Penn	BETTY
Isaac Thomas	THE ALPHA
Richard Stoutt	PILGRIM
Richard Stoutt	SAFETY/LEDA P
Maxwell Lettsome	STUDY/ PARHAMTOWN/ WASP
Anthony Stoutt	UNION
Wilfred Penn	DARLING
James Smith, Leah Smith Haldane Davies Richard Stoutt	FOUR FRIENDS (motor launch)
Carris Penn	DELMAN/LIBERTY

VIRGIN GORDA	
Rufus Walters	CEDAR BRANCH/BRINDICATE
James A. Stevens	RONILDA
Howard O'Neal	CONCORD/SWIFT KEEL/MAYWORD
Robinson O'Neal	MARRIS
Elvin Flax	ANEGADA/FLYING ARROW
Leopold Walters	PETREL
Gerald Walters	MOSQUITO
Edgar Walters	PACIFICO
Alfred Vanterpool	ROSALIND
Osmond Stevens	SIGNET
James N. Vanterpool	WILL WONDER
Allan O'Neal	FLYING ARROW
Edwin Wheatley, Cecil Rhymer	MAYBE
Oharra Harrigan	MARY M *(MOUNTAIN MARY
Evermond Rabsatt	
J. R. O'Neal	

SEA COWS BAY	
James "Jinna" Smith	REINDEER
Adolphus Rawleigh	ELSIE
Owen Smith	REINDEER
Canute Frazer	LILY
Richard Mactavious	VIGILATE
BAUGHERS BAY	
Walter Malone, Ernest Pickering	THE EDEN/ LADY P
Owen Maduro & Amos Hodge	THE WONDER WHY
The Family of J.E.W. Georges	THE WONDER WHY (owners)
Samuel Freeman	AJAX/NEPTUNE
Ernest Pickering	JOAN OF ARC
Ernest Pickering	EMPRESS
ROAD TOWN	
Leopold Smith	TYFON/VIRGIN ISLANDER
Carlton Decastro	TINY LOU/BELLS OF ST. MARY
John James LaFong	MERRIX
Ludrick Smith	UNITY/BLUE PETER
Bruce Family	BLUE PETER (OWNERS)
James Alfred Skelton	ESMIE
H.M. Government	LADY KATE
BELLE VUE	
Samuel Malone	CONSOLATION
WEST END	
John Hyman	THE FOAM
John, Arthur, Henry Hodge	THE HILDA
Benjamin & Joseph Romney	THE FLAME
The Ronan Family	THE IDLER
Ensor Smith	ANNA/ETHLYN
Benjamin A. Romney	VICUNA/ELSIE/ISLANDER
Solomon Hyman	EARLY BIRD

Daniel Smith	ELSA
John Amos Delville	ELLA/DARLING
Alexander "Morsa" Leonard	OLYMPIA/DAHOME
CARROT/CAPPOONS/LITTLE APPLE BAYS	
Osmond Donovan	BRITTANIA
Antonio Donovan	GUIANA/MYSTERY
Samuel Smith	STARLIGHT
Sonny Scatliffe	ILVA
John Callwood	FAITH
Samuel "Sammie" Callwood	VALENCIA
Victor Callwood	LADY ENA
James & Herman Donovan	LINDA
King Donovan & William Ronan	THE IDLER
Leslie Donovan	PRIZE
Rufus Callwood	ESPERANZA
Austin Callwood	STRANGER
Lucas Donovan	ETHLYN
Donald Smith	ROSALINA
James & Alexander Smith	FANCY ME
Sammie Callwood	MAY
CANE GARDEN BAY	
Rudolph Hodge	PRIDE OF TORTOLA
Rudolph & Allan Hodge	HAVANA
Louis & Richard Callwood	DIXIE
Morris Martin	NERISSA/DAISY
Monroe "Sonny" Henley	CONSOLATION
Harrigan Family	SPEEDWELL
EAST END (Additions)	
Archibald Smith & Milton Thomas	CAUTION/TEMPER/TINTA BELL
James Lettsome	OLIVE
Bernard & Osmond Penn	ENERGY/SOCIAL (SOLD TO*)
Henry Vanterpool	SECRET
William Frett	SOCIAL
Richard Penn	DARLING (SOLD TO*)

Chris Penn	DARLING
Timothy Frett & Osmond Davies	LAUREL
Henry Penn	BRITTON #I
Fritz Penn	PALOMA BIRD/BRITTON #II
Wilfred Penn	BRITTON

(BRITTON #II was sold to Desmond Holdridge, author of "Escape to the Tropics." In his book Holdridge gives an account of the sale, description of the boat and the journey back to St. John where he then lived.)

"The Fancy Me"

The early years of the twentieth century were a very difficult time for the people of the British Virgin Islands. Work was very hard to come by and men of the colony had to cast their eyes outward in the quest to earn a living for themselves and their families.

At that time the growing sugar industries of the former Spanish colonies of Cuba, Puerto Rico and especially the Dominican Republic (then known as Santo Domingo) were suffering from an acute shortage of available labour. The wages offered were above and beyond what anyone would earn in the English-speaking Island to east and it was not long before the call for workers was answered. From all the Leeward Islands they went and from all the Virgin Islands, British or Danish.

Employed originally as seasonal workers, several of these intrepid souls settled in the host countries permanently. However most returned home at the end of each "sugar season" and bided their time until recruits were again needed Boats that carried all kinds of cargoes (including men) plied a lively and regular trade between the small islands and what one Tortolian called :the vast continent of Santo Domingo," but referred to simply as "the land". Families in the British Virgin Islands eagerly awaited the arrival of these "schooners" which would bring remittances from the workers, or would reunite them with their loved ones. Although many navigated the voyages without incident, the journey from San Pedro de Macoris to Road Town what is still considered by many as the worst tragedy in the B.V.I history The "Fancy Me".

The "Fancy Me" was a schooner built in St. Thomas and was owned by the brothers James and Alexander Smith of Carrot Bay. Although largely a cargo boat the "Fancy Me" had a passenger capacity of some 100. It travelled between Tortola, St. Thomas and the Dominican Republic.

On the July 25, 1926, the "Fancy Me" was returning from the port of San Pedro de Macoris, where most of the Virgin Islanders worked. The list of passengers included Anegradians and Tortolians; for the Tortolians, it was a trip eagerly anticipated, as it would coincide with the celebration of August 1'st. Unfortunately, this reunion was not to be.

The voyage to Tortola from Macoris presented few terrors to experienced seamen like Captain James Smith of the "Fancy Me" when the weather was good. However, when the boats along with several other schooners mainly from Anguilla, set sail the "Hurricane season" was well underway.

After one day's sailing the boats were caught in a storm and captains took shelter between the Dominican Republic and Saona – a small island just south of Hispaniola. Unfortunately Captain Smith had stored his heavy anchor under a shipment of sugar (also destined for Tortola and of sufficient quality to satisfy the needs of that island for the rest of the year). The lighter anchor which the captain employed to secure his vessel was not up to the mark and the "Fancy Me" broke free from its moorings and was wrecked on a rock known as "El Caballo Blanco" or "The White Horse".

The "Fancy Me" carried only one lifeboat. This was quickly launched by the crew and they clambered aboard, leaving the 89 passengers to fend for themselves. The latter attempted to get to land as best they could, grabbing hold of their wooden trunks, the hatches of the boat and bits of timber. Some made it to the shore but 59 men in the prime of their lives perished not a few of them providing the sharks with an unexpected meal.

Those who were eventually saved swam to Saona and waited for a passing boat. The first boat that approached was a small one and there was chaos as all tried to force their way onto it. After persuasion that was generally emphasized by violence or threats thereof, those passengers who had not yet boarded the boat decided to stay on the island until the arrival of another one. The survivors were taken to the Dominican town of La Romana where, it is said, several included themselves with money taken from the less fortunate.

When the small boat bringing the first group of survivors arrived in Tortola, it was met by a large number of persons awaiting the return of their relatives. On hearing the sad news all were overcome by grief, some to the extent of fainting.

Of those who returned alive from the ill-starred voyage of the "Fancy Me" only a few are still with us. They are now men who have lived their "threescore and ten" years or more and include Mr. Leonell Donovan of Carrot Bay and Mr. James Connor of Road Town.

The "Fancy Me" was not the first nor the last boat from the British Virgin Islands to be wrecked at sea but long after the others have been forgotten by all but historians, the loss of the "Fancy Me" will remain etched indelibly in the memories of the children and grandchildren of those affected by the British Virgin Islands worst sea tragedy.

THE "SEINE BOAT" OWNED BY ARCHIBALD HODGE OF FRENCHMAN'S CAY

LOSS OF THE SCHOONER "FANCY ME"

1. A schooner named the "Fancy Me"
   Was scudding in gale.
   She ran before a raging sea
   With neatly shortened sail.

2. She had aboard Tortola's sons
   Returning home again.
   Her cargo was just fifteen tons
   Of sugar from the cane.

3. The captain saw a storm was on No
   haven was in sight.
   So long a wooden isle he won'
   No deep intended bight.

4. He anchored in an open road
   The scene of many a wreck.
   And thinking of his precious load
   He slowly paced the deck.

5. He looked upon the rising moon
   No weather glass had he.
   "A hurricane is coming soon
   Alas my Fancy Me".

6. The fated schooner's handsome shape
   Was sheltered by the land.
   The billows at Espada's cape
   Were raging on the strand.

7. A heavy swell struck "Fancy Me"
   Her iron cable rent.
   Before the gale far out to sea
   The hapless vessel went.

8. The sailors rigged a floating kedge
   To keep her head to sea.
   She sped on like a driven wedge
   As helpless as she could be.

9. The wind blew veered round due south it blew
And drove her back to land.
She struck a rock as near as she drew
With all her mottled band.

10. The captain perished with his trust
As only hero dies
And in Saona's clayery dust
His mouldering body lies.

(From the unpublished works of Mr. Alphaeus Osario Norman 1885 - 1942)

The Wreck of the Perseverance (to insert- Straight From Us Vol 2 –check for 13 names)

It was a Monday morning and everything seemed normal except for the wind. There wasn't enough breeze to blow a grass straw boat in a pond, much less to move the local boats which were laden with cargo bound for St. Thomas.

It was usual thing for the captains to "clear" their boats at West End the evening before the day of the actual voyage, so they could begin the voyage to St. Thomas during the fore-day morning.

The Wonder Why, Daisy, Consolation, Perseverance, and Guyana began their journey that morning, under oar power. The Wonder Why, I.E.W. Georges' boat was ahead of the fleet. Following was the Daisy which belonged to the Martins of Soldier Hill. The Consolation, the Henley boat from Cane Garden Bay, was third or about ten minutes behind the Daisy. The Perseverance and the Guyana were so far behind that we couldn't see them during the journey down the Ghut. I was on the Consolation.

When we reached Whistling Islands a light breeze sprang out of the north and the oar men welcomed it with open arms. They put the oars across. Stephen May was the most feared area in The Ghut. It was and still is famous for its heavy rollers and strong tides. By the time the Consolation reached Stephen May a strong wind was blowing from the north and the boat was really moving. The Daisy was still ahead. The narrowest areas down The Ghut are called the Wonder Why Passage. By the time we reached there, the wind had become so strong that Sonny Henley, my great uncle, told his nephew Manny Henley, my father, to reef the sails. Manny did not agree with his experienced Uncle Sonny. Looking at the weather, my father said, "Let's take her as much as she can, we have to make time." If the sails are permitted to take in too much wind the mast could be over pressured and collapse.

We kept a strict eye on the wind pressure, on the sails and mast. Meanwhile the weather was getting worse. Old uncle Sonny Henley warned his nephew again to reef the sails, but he refused, once more saying, "We have to make time. Let her rip!"

As we approached Long Point we could look straight ahead at Signal Hill and we saw that a gale warning was posted. We entered Charlotte Amalie harbor. The wind was blowing from many angles. We were now forced to reef and tack until we finally made it to the wharf. Wonder Why and Daisy had docked just minutes ahead.

From the wharf we looked toward the Harbour Mouth and saw a sloop which no doubt was from the B.V.I. It was Perseverance. It came into the harbour but could not make it to the dock. The wind was driving it away toward the south. Minutes later, only a white smoke-like foam could be seen as the wind whipped up the water. The boat vanished into the white smoke-like mist. The Harbour Master issued an order, telling the captains to take their boats down to the Mudhole. This was a protective area nearby where they could ride out the storm.

The Storm passed and another day had begun. Everyone was concerned about the lives that no doubt were lost on the boat that had come inside the habour mouth and disappeared. The harbour patrol went out to sea. No trace of the Perseverance was seen.

Remember that another boat called Guyana was making the same trip, but was far behind. The boat belonged to the late Rudolph Hodge (Dulphié). He was so far behind because he took on cargo at Brewers Bay, Tortola and it took him longer to pull from Cane Garden Bay to West End to be cleared. His boat the Guyana was caught in the gale too and could not make it inside the Harbour Mouth due to the strong north winds. Dulphié, being a man of courage and wit, felt his boat being driven south and decided to beach it on Buck Island. He and all his crew were saved, and were picked up after the gale.

Elmore Stoutt interviewed
James Henley of Cane Garden Bay

George Janial Tomau
Joe Tomau
Sandy McClean & Two Sons
Willie Smith
Samuel Tomau
Clarke Tomau
Jake Tomau
Little John
Ellen Frett
Daniel Venzen
Joseph Pickering

Emigrants from Tortola to Dominican Republic, April 1930

From VICO # 71929

Emigrant		Sex	Residence	Destination	Deposit
William	Smith	Male	East End Tortola	Sto: Domingo	1 5 0
George	Donavon	do	Sage Mountain	do do	1 5 0
Edmund	Arundel	do	Anegada	do do	1 5 0
Leroy	Wheatley	do	Anegada	do do	1 5 0
Maxwell	Maduro	do	Road Town	do do	1 5 0
Theophilus	Fahie	do	Long Trench	do do	1 5 0
Irvine	Donavon	do	Road Town	do do	1 5 0
Joseph	Tomar	do	East End	do do	1 5 0
David	Daniel	do	Road Town	do do	1 5 0
Alfred	Jennings	do	Huntumn's Gut	do do	1 5 0
Daniel	Turnbull	do	Harrigan's	do do	1 5 0
Franklyn	Phillip	do	Meyers'	do do	1 5 0
Samuel	Robinson	do	Harrigan's	do do	1 5 0
Eric	Callwood	do	Meyers'	do do	1 5 0
John S	Hodge	do	Cane Garden Bay	do do	1 5 0
Henry	Hodge	do	do do do	do do	1 5 0
Osmaond	Brathwaite	do	Meyers'	do do	1 5 0
Samuel	Hodge	do	Cane Garden Bay	do do	1 5 0
Benjamin	Industrios	do	Meyers'	do do	1 5 0
John	Potter	do	Doty's	do do	1 5 0
David	Smith	do	Meyers'	do do	1 5 0
Henry	Adams	do	Challwill's	do do	1 5 0
Charles	Francis	do	Harrigan's	do do	1 5 0
Antonio	Williams	do	Joes Hill	do do	1 5 0
David	Turnbull	do	Meyers'	do do	1 5 0
Benjamin	Todman	do	do	do do	1 5 0
Samuel	Woods	do	do	do do	1 5 0
Richard	Penn	do	East End	do do	1 5 0
Edward	Smith	do	do do	do do	1 5 0
Antonio	Wheatley	do	do do	do do	1 5 0
Charles	Penn	do	do do	do do	1 5 0
Claude	Wheatley	do	do do	do do	1 5 0
Eric	Smith	do	do do	do do	1 5 0
Joseph	Smith	do	do do	do do	1 5 0
Wellington	Rymer	do	Soldier Hill	do do	1 5 0
Oliver	Penn	do	East End	do do	1 5 0
William	Leonard	do	Soldier Hill	do do	1 5 0
Ira	Ham	do	Road Towh	do do	1 5 0
Daniel	Brathwaite	do	Leonards'	do do	1 5 0
Alexander	Leonard	do	Carrot Bay	do do	1 5 0
James A.	Francis	do	Harrigan's	do do	1 5 0
Sydney	Jennings	do	Huntumn's Gut	do do	1 5 0
Maurice	Ham	do	Baughers Bay	do do	1 5 0
Alfred	Vanterpool	do	Road Town	do do	1 5 0
William	Smith	do	Carrot Bay	do do	1 5 0
Leo	Barry	do	Pleasant Valley	do do	1 5 0
Altimon	Matthias	do	Seacow's Bay	do do	1 5 0
Daniel	Matthias	do	do	do do	1 5 0
William	King	do	do	do do	1 5 0
David	Matthias	do	do	do do	1 5 0
Alexander	Cills	do	do	do do	1 5 0
John	Thomas	do	do	do do	1 5 0
Alexander	Turnbull	do	do	do do	1 5 0
William	Hodge	do	do	do do	1 5 0
Clifford	Callwood	do	Turnbull's	do do	1 5 0
Albert	Smith	do	Seadowds Bay	do do	1 5 0

Emigrants from Tortola, B.V.I.
to 31st Mar: 1930

EMIGRANT	SEX	RESIDENCE	DESTINATION	AMT: DEPOSOTED		
Joseph Knight	Male	Anegada	Sto. Domingo	1	5	0
Samuel Francis	do	Road Town	do	1	5	0
John Jackman	do	Anegada	do	1	5	0
John V. Vanterpool	do	do	do	1	5	0
Wilbert Faulkner	do	do	do	1	5	0
Ephraim Smith	do	Meyers Tort:	do	1	5	0
Elridge Robinson	do	do	do	1	5	0
Isadore Dunlop	do	Anegada	do	1	5	0
James Knight	do	do	do	1	5	0
Semi-Sustin Knight	do	do	do	1	5	0
Emile Dunlop	do	do	do	1	5	0
Gustave F. Norman	do	do	do	1	5	0
George Christopher	do	Anderson Tor:	do	1	5	0
Arnold Vanterpool	do	Anegada	do	1	5	0
Olva Rymer	do	do	do	1	5	0
Amos Hodge	do	Free Bottom Tor:	do	1	5	0
Hubert Wells	do	Anegada	do	1	5	0
Ivan Godfrey	do	Long Trench Tor:	do	1	5	0
Sydney Maduro	do	Baugher's Bay	do	1	5	0
James Martin	do	Brewers Bay	do	1	5	0
Felix Smith	do	Long Trench	do	1	5	0
Reuben Downing	do	Belle Vue	do	1	5	0
Irvine Dawson	do	Brewers Bay	do	1	5	0
Emanuel Mercer	do	Baughers Bay	do	1	5	0
Isaiah Smith	do	Belle Vue	do	1	5	0
Rudolph Jennings	do	do do	do	1	5	0
James Christopher	do	Brewers Bay	do	1	5	0
Thomas Scatliffe	do	Belle Vue	do	1	5	0
Arthur Rogers	do	Anegada	do	1	5	0
Alexander Jennings	do	Belle Vue	do	1	5	0
Reuben Ham	do	Free Bottom	do	1	5	0
Ella Albertha Carey	Female	Road Town	do	1	5	0
Thomas Dawson	Male	Carrot Bay	do	1	5	0
Charles Donavon	do	do do	do	1	5	0
John Frett	do	Long Look	do	1	5	0
Alexander Williams	do	Joes Hill	do	1	5	0
David Scatliffe	do	Fahie Hill	do	1	5	0
James Freeman	do	do do	do	1	5	0
Dennis Potter	do	East End	do	1	5	0
Arthur Frett	do	do do	do	1	5	0
Thomas Potter	do	do do	do	1	5	0
Maxwell Lettsome	do	do do	do	1	5	0
Leo Frett	do	Long Trench	do	1	5	0
Alexander Todman	do	Georges' N. Side	do	1	5	0
Western Phillips	do	Meyers	do	1	5	0
William Frett	do	East End	do	1	5	0
Clarence Lettsome	do	Long Look	dd	1	5	0
Naaman Rabsatt	do	Long Look	do	1	5	0
James Stephens	do	Major Bay	do	1	5	0
George Callwood	do	Turnbull's	do	1	5	0
Irvine Frett	do	Major Bay	do	1	5	0
Irvine Freeman	do	Fahie Hill	do	1	5	0
Charles Todman	do	Georges' N. Side	do	1	5	0
George I. Turnbull	do	Great Mountain	do	1	5	0
James Vanterpool	do	Fahie Hill	do	1	5	0
Chas V. Christopher	do	Georges' N. Side	do	1	5	0
James Frett	do	Long Trench	do	1	5	0
Daniel Fleming	do	do do	do	1	5	0
Osmond Hetherington	do	do do	do	1	5	0
Alcidas Vanterpool	do	Fahie Hill	do	1	5	0
Gustave Vanterpool	do	do do	do	1	5	0
Charles Jennings	do	Hope Hill	do	1	5	0

CRAFTS

AND

SKILLS

HANDED

DOWN

Skills Handed Down

Several of our citizens travelled to Santo Domingo during the early part of this century and brought back with them many skills which were utilized in the various communities. During the early days, the apprenticeship system required each boy and girl to learn a trade. Through this system, the skills of older generations were passed on to the younger. Some of the skills and skilled workers are mentioned below.

The brothers, Joshua and Alfredo Crabbe, Mr. Silva and Cyril Baronville were skilled tinsmiths. They made cups from cans on which handles were soldered. These were known as "can cups" and there was not a home in the Territory without a "tin cup". These men were also able to make milk pans and water pans called "brickers". A "bricker" was the cylindrical tin drum in which water was carried on donkeys.

Mr. Charles "Wally" Smith was an excellent stone mason. His houses and brick ovens were indeed works of art.

Ezekiel Malone of Long Swamp designed a mill for the sole purpose of grinding arrowroot. This was done in the 1940's. It consisted of two giant rollers on which graters were placed. The arrowroot was placed between the rollers and these were then turned by hand. The juice from the arrowroot was allowed to dry and was used as starch; the ground stalk was used as cattle feed. The dried arrowroot juice was also used as a cereal called "souloup". This was used as a cereal usually at times of illness when it was suspected that the patient had a "weak stomach" and needed "soft" food. To be so sick that "you could only drink 'souloup'" was to be sick indeed. The largest fields of arrowroot were grown at Spring Ghut although many homes had their own small plots of arrowroot. Ezekiel Malone (Butcher) designed hampers from local withes for the Guana Island resort in the fifties.

The art of sewing and embroidery was taught by many women to young girls. Mrs. Leona O'Neal Harney, Mrs. Floressa Lettsome, Virginia Parrott Fahie, Geraldine Ritter, Blanche Pickering, Vivian Donovan Hetherington - now of St. Thomas, all passed on sewing and embroidery skills to girls in the areas where they lived. Many homes sported beautiful pieces of Teneriffe, hardanger, Spanish drawn thread work and other forms of embroidery brought to the territory by people from outside or learned by British Virgin Islanders outside and brought in.

Paraquin Lace making was introduced in the 1890's by Alberta Brodie. She hailed from Belgium and purchased Beef Island where she lived for many years. She taught young ladies of East End the craft and this was for them a source of income. Among the young ladies in the East End area who were very good at this thread weaving on frames were:

Amantis Smith-Varlack
Cecile Penn
Beulah Frett-Brodie
Edith Frett
Iva Varlack
Eda Varlack-Flax

This skill spread from one village to the other and finally there were many women and girls in the territory who were experts at the art of needle weaving.

THOMAS LLOYD, father of Eva Amelia Lloyd of East End introduced the craft of hat weaving and this was a skill he acquired in Santo Domingo. At that time all tyre straw came from Santo Domingo, but in later years the white tyre came from St. Barts. The brown "broom" tyre was acquired from Guana Island and St. John. Some skilled straw workers of note included:

Violet Gore	Catherine Lettseome	Evangeline Malone Leah
Exzeria Penn	Henriette Stevens	Smith
Heino Stevens	Marie Durante Wheatley	Clotilda O. Penn

* (Heino Stevens—father of Dr. Joel Stevens—transported the items of straw-work for sale to persons on St. John, St. Croix and St. Thomas and was indeed the retailer for the people of East End/Long Look).

During the wars many of the school rooms were swept with brooms made of maran-bush. Industrious and handy men like:

Walter Penn
Leopold Penn
Butcher Malone

learned the craft of making brooms with or without sticks. These they made in their spare time and the straw was obtained from Guana Island. The brooms are still popular in the village and are often referred to by other villagers as the "East End ole time broom".

Jennie N. Wheatley

DARWIN SCATLIFFE AND HIS BASKETS
A GREAT OLD TIMER

The Art of straw work a Way of Life

INTRODUCTION

The craft of hat weaving was first introduced in the 1800s to the people of the British Virgin Islands (BVI) by a gentleman named Mr. Thomas Lloyd, the father of Ms. Eva Amelia Lloyd of East-End. Mr. Lloyd acquired this skill while living in Santo Domingo. At that time, all straw Teyer came from Santo Domingo, and, in later years, the white Teyer came from St. Bartholomew. The brown "broom" Teyer was obtained either free of cost or purchased from Guana Island, Scrub Island, St. John and St. Thomas. Mr. Walter Penn was the person who supplied the broom Teyer from Guana Island. In the days when straw work was active and thriving, people depended heavily on it both for their livelihood and to strengthen community ties. This art has passed down through the generations via our forefathers who learnt the skill and passed it on to their children. In some way, our parents, grandparents and our great-grandparents all had a part to play in the production of straw work. In most cases, the straw workers had assistance from family members in some way, either great or small. Some participated in cutting and transporting the Teyer, some in plaiting the splits and even sewing the plaits into products for sale.

These items were first sewn by hand before sewing machines were available demonstrating how people of that time used whatever means they had to support themselves and their families.

NAMES ASSOCIATED WITH THE STRAW WORK INDUSTRY

The names of a few people recognized for their straw

working skills include Mrs. Violet Gore, Mrs. Lucia Crabbe-Penn, Mrs. Elzeria Penn, Mrs. Catherine Lettsome, Mrs. Marie Durante Wheatley, Mrs. Clotilda O.

Penn, Mr. Heino Stevens, Mrs. Henrietta Stevens, Mrs. Evangeline Malone, Mrs. Amabel Malone-Frett, Mrs. Leah Smith, Mrs. Estelle Dawson, and Mrs. Amanda Malone. Mr. Heino Stevens, the father of Dr. Joel Stevens, transported many of the items made from straw such as hats and baskets for sale to persons on St. John, St. Croix, and St. Thomas, where he was known as the retailer for the people of East End and Long Look.

Mrs. Jennie Wheatley fondly recalled vivid memories of the people long ago who were involved in various aspects of straw work . She remembers that at any time of the day you could find people busy plaiting splits, drying Teyer, dyeing splits, pressing plaits or sewing hats and bags. The main market for the finished products was in the United States Virgin Islands, be it St. John, St. Croix. Before that, the items were sent (as we say down island) to St. Kitts and Antigua by weekly sailing sloops captained by our very own captains such as Mr. Joseph Smith, Mr. Dennis Potter and Mr. Milford Chauvell. On their return they would bring sugar, ground provisions and money from the sales made. Even though the straw work was time consuming, the ladies still found time to engage in other skills such as sewing clothing, baking bread and pastries, and housekeeping. The people of the community helped each other. Whilst some persons could only plait splits, they could take them to another person to sew on items for them or to add some sort of finishing touch. If a person was unable to add some sort of special design to a hat, they would simply get it done by someone else who could.

When church hats were scarce during the Second World War (1939-45), the locally made hats were in great demand to meet the need. This type of hat was made with a certain flair. Mrs. Leah Smith was very instrumental in this area. The hats were produced in red, green and yellow colors, as they could match most dresses. A variety of colours were made.

The Government's Senior Citizens Programme, administered through the Social Development Department, provides an opportunity for senior citizens of the East-End and Long Look communities to continue to enjoy their skills making various types of craft, including items made of straw. Some of the seniors participate by plaiting splits, whilst some of the ladies sew the items together. Hats produced by the seniors of this programme have won prizes at some of the annua Farmer's Week exhibitions.

TERMINOLOGY

Splits - The pieces of dried Teyer for plaiting.

Plait - Splits woven together.

Plaiting - The process of weaving the splits to produce a pattern or plait.

Trimming - Removing the unwanted or protruding straw or splits from the plait.

Pressing - The use of a clothes iron to make the plaits smooth and straight.

Dyeing - The process of adding colour to the straw.

PRODUCTION PROCESS

The first stage is to cut the closed Teyer from the tree upon which it grows. The Teyer must then be laid in the sun on both sides until it is fully dried. The Teyer should never get wet, as this makes it unusable. The water stains and changes the colour of the straw and it develops mildew. To assist in this process, the leaves are pared out or separated allowing the drying process to accelerate. The leaves are then cut from the main base ready for making splits which vary according

Market stall displaying stra ware Photo by M.M. Barzey-Penn

to the desired product or pattern. For example, the splits for making hats are smaller than those used for making baskets.

Left Column
Market stall displaying straw ware Photo by M.M. Barzey-Penn
Once the splits are ready, the pattern is determined and the process of plaiting begins.

PATTERNS

Of the various types of plaits used for making hats, the eleven split was the most popular. Others were the five split, seven split, the fifteen split, and the twenty-one split. The really skilled straw workers also produced 'hole in the middle' or 'X in the middle', the 'insertion' and the very creative 'saw teeth' designs. The method of plaiting the five split is one over, under one, until the desired length of plait is completed. The method of plaiting the seven split is one over one, under two, until the desired length of the plait is achieved.

BOTTLE COVERING

Apart from the main industry of making hats, bags and baskets, another area explored was the covering of bottles with straw. The bottles, covered with straw, are very appealing and during the 1950's, a market existed in St. Thomas for the production of covered bottles. It is said that the Marketing Director of a perfume company had the idea that a bottle of cologne adorned in matted straw would be the best way to sell the product all over the world. And so, the manufacture of the cologne turned to the Virgin Islands for the straw covered bottles. The bottles were supplied in cases to be covered.

The BVI got a piece of the action when Mr. Ebert Lettsome of East End became the local agent and soon established himself as a competent seaman. He took his crew aboard his thirty foot Tortola Sloop called *The Lower Lights* and transported many cases of bottles back and forth.

When Mr. Lettsome returned from St. Thomas, he would bring along bails of white straw to sell for the work of covering the bottles he brought. His home, which was located in the Parham Town valley, became the storage and distribution centre. In those days, there were no vehicles in East End, and men had to carry cases of bottles on their shoulders, about a five minute walk down to the boat at the wharf. This would have been the only role these men would have played in the industry. The skill of covering bottles with straw was known as 'knitting the bottles' and this was done solely by women.

Mr. Lettsome would train interested persons. In those days, almost every household in the East End, Fat Hog's Bay and Long Look areas was engaged in straw work. Women would go to Mr. Lettsome's house for their assigned work: cases containing 36 or 48 four ounce, eight ounce or eighteen ounce bottles were given to the ladies to cover within a certain time frame. Depending on their ability, two or three cases were handed out at a time. The ladies would purchase their own straw from Mr. Lettsome and were paid $6.00 for each four ounce case of bottles, $8.00 for each eight ounce case of bottles and $10.00 for each sixteen ounce case of bottles.

This type of work was in high demand and a high standard was expected. If a bottle was not neatly dressed, clean or properly tailored, it would be rejected and a reduction would be made from the cost of labour. It must be noted that there are four stages in the production of knitted bottles as follows:

1. 'Setting the bottles'. This means that a person would prepare the fish eye or fish port pattern on her work table to the specified formula.
2. 'Framing the bottle'. The person would then fit the matting to the bottle. Here was the real test of the skill, for the socket not only had to fit snuggly, but it had to be strengthened at points by overlays which were not obvious.
3. 'Trimming the bottles'. Here the person would clip all ends protruding and dust off the bottles.
4. The cases were then returned to Mr. Lettsome's house.

In the mid-1960's, Mr. Lettsome gave up his role and there was great difficulty finding a competent replacement for him. Finally in recent years, a reliable person was found as his replacement.

Today, the practice of the craft is still the woman's domain but the earnings are slightly higher than that of yesteryear. It is also said that as long as the West Indian Bay Rum Company still survives and a local agent can be found, the united States Virgin Islands (USVI) will continue to attract this skill in straw work.

Mrs. Zelia Frett still makes covers for the bottles today with the 'fish pot' design. She learnt this skill from her older sister, Mrs. Valaria Wheatley during her school days. From her many years of experience, Mrs. Frett prepares the socket from the base without having to use a flat surface anymore. Today, Mrs. Frett covers bottles for the local spice factory, 'Sunny Caribe'. She has been working on her own covering bottles for them for over a year. For many years though she worked with Mrs. Cassilda Potter and others covering bottles for the same company. She says that she acquires the white Teyer from the French people in St. Thomas who grow the trees that produce the straw.

MRS. AMANDA MALONE'S EXPERIENCE WITH STRAW WORK

Mrs. Amanda Malone (affectionately known as Ms. Manda to the

Man's hat by Miss Manda Photo by M.M. Barzey-Penn

community) and as 'Granny' to her children, grandchildren, and great-grandchildren), is 74 years old and can recall making hats from the age of fifteen years old. Ms. Manda, like many others, started sewing hats by hand and then later learned how to do them by sewing machine. She also had a talent sewing clothing from that tender age. In later years, Ms. Manda migrated to St. Thomas where she worked for a hotel. She never however gave up her straw work which she continued during her spare time in the evening. She recalls whilst living in St. Thomas that she would get up early in the morning and sew five women's hats from the straw she had plaited the night before, then set off to her full time job at the hotel.

Her husband, Mr. Daniel Malone (affectionately known as 'Shady'), and her children assisted her with plaiting the straw strips, from which she would sew together such items as hats, mats, baskets called 'macoto' or 'saccou', and caps. Ms. Amanda also made bone baskets from the bone or hard portion of the white Teyer and soft splits woven in between the bones. She remembers how well Mrs. Lou Gordon made bone baskets. Ms. Manda taught all of her children how to plait straw from a young age. They would even race amongst themselves to see how much straw each person could plait in a given time. Mr. Malone learned how to plait from childhood also but could only plait the five strip. He recalls using the leaves from coconut trees for practice. Ms. Manda has been asked to teach the craft to people on occasion but says now that the young people do not have much interest in learning the skill. In fact, their parents seemed to be the ones who show the most interest.

Women's hat by Miss Manda Photo by M.M. Barzey-Penn

Mr. Malone would go over to St. Thomas and St. John each week with as many as 100 items for sale which consisted of hats, bags, baskets, different types of mats and coasters, all made by his wife. He would leave on Friday mornings and return on the Saturday or the Sunday with the money from the successful sales. His very best customer was a company in St. John from whom he collected a sure cheque each time. This customer has since been passed on to Mrs. Luella Crabbe-Penn when Ms. Malone retired from his days of hustling. The straw work had been made into a family business and was their main source of income for some time. Ms. Manda mentioned that they purchased plaited straw by the yard from other persons in the community in order to assist the family which contributed to the 100 items they created each week. She remembers paying various prices for the plaited straw according to the design.

Mr. Malone also recalls other people from Tortola following him to St. Thomas of some of their merchandise to sell but he caught on to them and did not tell them who his customers were. He said that there were people who wanted to steal his business and undermine him but that he would wait until the afternoon to to avoid attention. Mr. Malone remembers on two occasions when he took some hats to St. Thomas to sell, but his customers did not require them. One of these times he remembers saying to himself that he would sell those hats "in the name of the Father the Son and the Holy Ghost." Soon after walking down the road, he met someone who subsequently purchased all of the hats he had. On another occasion, he could remember a lady by the name of Mrs. Adora Verzon who paid him for his hats and held them until his customers required them to whom in turn, she would sell them .

Mrs. Manda also did a little bit of selling herself and she spoke about some experiences with other ladies who also made straw work their livelihood. She mentioned that a lady from Fat Hog's Bay played tricks and displayed acts of selfishness back in the day because of the competition. There was a white lady who came regularly to purchase items from an area in Hodge's Creek where the local ladies sold their merchandise. There was one woman who wanted the white lady to buy from only her, but the white lady's policy was that as long as a person's product was good, she would buy from anybody. She said, "everybody has to eat." Mrs. Manda also spoke about money she was unable to collect for items people took from her but never paid for.

Mrs. Manda mentioned that some of the ladies would take on the task of making hats for business people and then fall behind on their production. They would then come to her for help in meeting the demand. Through these experiences, Mrs. Manda's skill became well known. She recalls sewing twenty four children's hats in one day which left her exhausted. On another occasion she remembers making seventeen adult's hats in one day. Her men's hats took as much as twelve yards of plait and the ladies hats took ten to twelve yards, whilst children's hats only took about four yards to make.

Mrs. Manda could plait many different patterns and even invented a few styles of her own including the 'scallop', (a combination of nine or eleven split with a French end), and the 'all over braid' (a combination of patterns woven together). She spoke of having the ability to make items as the ideas came to her mind, or at her customer's request. To sew a hat, the crown must be formed first. There is a technique in doing this which involves forming the crown into a shape as you sew the plaits together. Mrs. Manda used pieces of cloth called 'madras' to adorn or band her hats.

Mrs. Edith Penn, Ms. Manda's first child, recalls her mother making special carnival hats for August Monday. Some of the hats had a cone shaped crown and the rim had loose splits hanging. She also remembers her mother winning prizes for the lovely hats of various designs which she had made for the annual Farmer's Week exhibitions. The last two hats Mrs. Malone recalls making were the ones for my husband David (her grandson) and I. A few years ago she took ill and has not been able to do any sewing since. She is concerned that straw work is not being kept alive as it should, and hopes that the Government will initiate a programme to preserve this wonderful skill. She thinks that more younger people ought to get involved and learn the skill in order to pass on the craft to the next generation.

MRS. ESTELLE DAWSON'S EXPERIENCE WITH STRAW WORK

Mrs. Estelle Dawson,

(affectionately known as Ms. Estelle), just recently celebrated her 86th birthday and has a legacy of producing straw items, mainly hats, for over 70 years. Ms. Estelle started making hats between the ages of 12-14 years. She was taught the skill by her mother, Mrs. Adela Eram, and recalls being so skilled at the craft that she even thought she rivaled her mother in presentation. Ms. Estelle later learned how to sew hats on the sewing machine and did so for both her mother and herself. Ms. Estelle was also a teacher from age 15-22 when she got married to Mr. Alexander (Elic) Dawson. She stopped teaching and soon began her career in straw work to make a living. She recalls making hats in her spare time after arriving home from her long days of teaching. Her husband would assist her in trimming the plaits and then take the hats to St. Thomas to sell. He would walk and walk until he had sold all of the hats. He did so well that she recalls being the first person to get as much as two dollars a hat. She remembers that happy day very clearly. As time progressed, the price on hats slowly rose higher and higher. Today, a single hat is sold for a price between $10 and $15. Ms. Estelle takes pride in the fact that she taught some of her daughters how to plait, to assist her in making hats. She remembers while still living in her mother's house before being married, that she used to send her hats to St. Croix by boat with Mr. Edward Fret and Mr. Austin Fret to sell and would receive 25 cents and sometimes 18 cents for a hat in those days. She also noted that around the same time, a pound of flour was one or two cents.

In the early days of hat making, Ms. Estelle would get the Teyer from St. Barths, Scrub Island, Guana Island, and from the French in St. Thomas. She started her process by drying the Teyer, separating it into splits, plaiting the straw strips, then trimming the protruding ends from the sections which were joined. She would then press the plaits on the right hand side and sew her hat. She started sewing the hat from the crown by first folding under a bit of the plait, stitching it down and then sewing in a circular fashion. "You leave some slack so that the hat would be shaped into the desired fashion as you continue sewing," Ms. Estelle proudly remarks.

DYING THE STRAW

Ms. Estelle dyes some of her white Teyer different colours, to either add a little colour to a hat or to mix and match colours. This is done by placing a pot of water onto the stove with a little salt until it boils. You then throw in the desired dye colour. Ms. Estelle pointed out that she has not been able to acquire the type of dye which was used in the past and now has to resort to the kind of dye used for dying clothes which she purchases from the supermarket. She also recalls using a five pound butter pan to boil the dye, heated over coal pits outside. After the straw is dyed it is hung to dry.

DESIGNS

Ms. Estelle used the eleven split to make hats for men and women. She can plait just about all designs or patterns except the 'X' or 'hole in the middle' pattern. She explained "when making hats, especially for men, a section of the crown has a row of X's in the middle plait which is useful for ventilation and minimizes sweating in the heat on a hot day." Since she does not plait this pattern she would ask another person to do it for her.

Ms. Estelle uses a piece of ribbon or cloth to adorn her hats. She makes hats of various designs such as saw teeth (zigzag), five split, eleven split, and six split insertion. The broom Teyer used to make the saw teeth hat must be very soft. She has made up to six hats a day and produced as many as 30 hats in one week. The plaiting process takes most of the time she says, and it can take several days to plait the few yards needed to make a hat, depending on the size. One of the Planter's (man's) hat could take as much as 18 yards with a lady's hat taking as much as 16 yards.

Ms. Estelle says that Ms. Marie Wheatley and herself are the only persons still alive in East End who can sew hats on a sewing machine. She also says that she was given the oppotunity to go to a school and display her skills to some students and made a hat for them in the two days that she was there. Ms. Estelle currently has hats on sale at Marlene Penn's health food restaurant in Road Town.

Along with hats, Ms. Estelle has made a variety of bags and baskets. She sews handbags onto a piece of cardboard to create the shape and form. She lines the inside with cloth and then neatens the ends before adding the handles. She finally adds a design onto the outside using raffia embroidery for decoration.

Ms. Estelle's son Carol told the author that he encouraged his mother to continue her skills to make a living after his father had passed away. He speaks of his experiences in obtaining the Broom Teyer for his mother from the nearby islands whilst he sailed around the region. He noticed that the broom Teyer trees grew almost exclusively on the north side or the most northerly parts of islands such as Guana Island, Scrub Island, Great Dog, Virgin Gorda, Mosquito Island, the Thatches, and the Camanoes. It would appear that they grow in rocky areas overhanging cliffs where they can be seen on the northern side of Tortola.

Carol learned how to cut the Broom Teyer from the trees and says you should only cut the closed stems as opened ones not be used for hat making. Only brooms can be made from the open stems as they have already been exposed to the sun. The Teyer is then put out to dry and opened by hand.

As well as hat making, Ms. Estelle and other skills which she used such as baking bread and pastries to be sold in her family's shop, located not far from where she lives overlooking Red Bay. This was another source of income for her family. She did not get involved in covering bottles but mentions that Mrs. Beulah Brodie, who is a skilled craftswomen in many aspects, could cover bottles beautifully with the fish pot design. She is concerned that the straw work trade is not being passed onto the younger generations and is worried that when the older folk who still use the skill pass on, the art will die with them. As Ms. Manda and Ms. Estelle have expressed, the straw work tradition needs to be kept alive in order to be passed to future generations. The industry in the past has been very important to the BVI and provided a source of income for many homes. With the advent of tourism, there is still a market for products made of straw and the art can still exist as an economically viable alternative to other careers. The pride that the straw workers take in their work expresses exactly how much it means to them as people, and there exists among them an inescapable joy in knowing that there is still interest in the art. Nothing gives them more pleasure than sharing their experiences.

REFERENCES

BVI Department of Education and Culture. 1984. *150 Years of Achievement 1824-1984.*

Wheatley, J. 2000 *A Walk Down Straw Work Memory Lane.*

Dawson, Estelle., Oral Interview Recorded at East End, Tortola-Sunday March 25th, 2001.

Malone, Amanda., Oral Interview Recorded at Long Look, Tortola-Sunday 11th March, 2001.

This paper was submitted by Myr Marzey-Penn, a native of Montserrat and resident of East End, Virgin Islands a graduate of the Myrla is also Studies Programme

CATHERINE JENNINGS MALONE

CAKE MAKER, FARMER

PHOTO TAKEN AT HER HOME IN LONG TRENCH WHILE SHE LOOKED DOWN ON HER FLOCK OF SHEEP.

Today I write my fondest memory of Paul Wattley, a photographer who paid attention to detail. Outside his old studio, east of the Post Office, I often pause and admire a photograph of Catherine Jennings Malone looking down on a flock of sheep in Long Trench. For almost ten years I begged Paul for that photograph and he always said yes, but never remembered to bring it. During his illness I told his daughter Mia about my request. I received the photograph a few days later. But I saw in the photograph then, I still see it now, but much clearer as experience has sharpened my vision. Catherine Jennings Malone, intelligent far-seeing eyes, patrician neck, strong hand needed by the farmer and cake maker par excellence, wayward plait sticking out from head tie a real plaid head tie, tied in the traditional manner. A big safety pin in one of her husband Sam's shirt or one of her son Roosevelt's shirt, speaks not of poverty but practicability. Her flowered, gathered skirt which would have fallen gracefully to her ankles shows a woman born in the late 19th century who lived a full life in the 20th century. Catherine's stick was there for support, but it was also a shepherd's stick for authority over and guidance over her sheep.

Paul Wattley, labelled this photograph TORTOLA WOMAN. I beg to suggest Virgin Islands woman, Caribbean woman or just woman.

Thank you for the legacy Paul.
Jennie N. Wheatley

POSTOR JOSHUA CRABBE OF THE APOSTOLIC FAITH LEARNED THE SKILL OF SOLDERING IN THE DOMINICAAN REPUBLIC. HE PASSED ON THE SKILL TO MANY OF HIS RELATIVES. ANN E. CRABBE BAKER FOR MANY YEARS. SHE SERVED EAST END AND LONG LOOK VILLAGES.

COAL PIT BURNING IS NOT A LOST ART. BEFORE THE DAYS OF ELECTRICITY, THE GOOSE NEVER FAILED, ALTHOUGH "POND WOOD" COAL WAS A BIT SLOW.

POT BREAD MAKING

IN THE DAYS WHEN "WOOD", "PEEL", AND "BLAST", WERE PASS WORDS IN THE BAKER'S HOUSEHOLD, THE OVEN WAS BUILT OF BRICKS AND CONCRETE, AND STOOD LIKE A CITADEL IN THE BACK YARD.

BUNDLES OF WOOD WERE BROUGHT FROM THE TICKETS YONDER, USUALLY ON THE HEADS OF THE MALE TEENAGERS, ONE OF TWO DAYS BEFORE THE BIG, BAKING DAY. THE BUSIEST BAKER BAKED TWICE OR THRICE PER WEEK, BUT FAMILY BAKING WAS USUALLY ONCE PER WEEK ON SATURDAYS.

TARTS, PUDDINGS, BISCUITS, BOYA, JOHNNY CAKES, AND LEAVEN BREAD WERE AMONG THE MANY GOODIES TURNED OUT.

THERE WAS A SPECIAL ART IN "LIGHTING THE OVEN", SO THAT THE WOOD BURNED WITH A CONSTANT GLOW. WHEN IT WAS ALL BURN DOWN, THE SPECIAL "OVEN STICK" WAS USED "TO STIR" THE COALS ENSURING THAT THE "BOTTOM" WAS WELL HEATED. COALS AND ASHES WERE SWEPT THROUGH THE "ASH PIT" WITH A MARAN BUSH BROOM, AND ITEMS WERE THEN GEOMETRICALLY PLACED WITH A LONG-HANDLED "PEEL".

THE OVEN TEMPERATURE WAS USUALLY HIGH ENOUGH FOR TWO BAKINGS: THE BREAD FIRST, FOLLOWED BY TARTS OR BISCUITS.

IT WAS THEN "BLASTED" (HEATED AGAIN) FOR PUDDINGS, BOYA OR CAKES.

WEDDINGS, BIRTHDAYS, CHRISTENINGS AND FESTIVE OCCASIONS WERE CHARACTERISED BY SPECIAL BAKINGS WHICH TURNED THE BAKER'S HOME INTO A COMMUNITY ACTION SCENE.

VERNA PENN-MOLL

LIBRARIAN

MRS. EDNA BLYDEN OF CANE GARDEN BAY AT THE OVEN—BREAD, TART, PUDDING CAKE

MISS L'THELMA THOMAS

MAKING OF CASSAVA BREAD

THEY

WERE

FIRST

CLASS

SPORTSMEN

FROM "CRICKET NOTES" BY CYRIL B. ROMNEY AS PUBLISHED IN THE APRIL 9, 1960 ISSUE OF THE "TORTOLA TIMES".

Dawson Passes

For several weeks OWEN DAWSON, a star cricketer, lay in a hospital ward suffering from a not too common complaint. His number was called on the morning of the 26th, and he passed on from local greatness to the great beyond. He was mourned by his fellow cricketers who walked beside his casket from the Peebles Hospital to the Methodist Cemetery at Springfield where they laid him in his final resting place. He now lies within a stone's throw of his favorite battleground, - indeed in a spot where he had driven many a soaring six during his very colourful career.

The vital statistics of DAWSON'S past are somewhat obscure but the fact that he became a legendary figure in local cricket during his lifetime is indicative of the performance of this man on his chosen field of battle. Whether it was "Madumbs", "Brother Woller", "Paddix", or Owen, his real name, whenever one of his many field names was uttered in cricket circles casual listeners became keen enthusiasts.

The Perfect All-Rounder

It appears that DAWSON entered the game as a youngster of about 15 sometime in the mid-thirties as a permanent fixture of the TORTOLA XI. From the start it became quite evident that he was possessed of unusual ability and was the island's version of the perfect allrounder. As a fielder, he played second fiddle only to ARTHUR MAC, that wizard in the slips. His left-handed open stance at the wicket netted the most prolific scores of his era and his left arm, around the wicket, pace bowling was the most deadly weapon an opponent could encounter. His accomplishment does not end here for after a long spell of bowling he would demand the wicket-keeper's pads and gloves, and hurry to the opposite end to put on a faultless display behind the stumps.

3 For You and 3 For Me

DAWSON either possessed a remarkable awareness of his own abilities or was the rarely encountered clairvoyant individual. It was in St. John in 1935 that Tortola was all out for 35 runs. Enquired 15-year old DAWSON, of his more mathematically inclined teammate, ARTHUR MAC, "What is the half of 35?" "Seventeen and a half," replied Mac. "Seventeen and a half's the limit," he snorted and upset St. John for 17, using a 4 ball 4 wicket hat trick to finish the match.

The late Laurie McKelly once boasted of his seven wickets for three runs accomplishment in one innings of a match. Team mate DAWSON wagered he would do likewise. That innings DAWSON'S bowling analysis showed seven wickets for three runs.

Later on in his career he encountered McGregor of St. Croix, a man who opened for his side and saw the fall of the 9th wicket. With one wicket to go, DAWSON faced his adversary and exclaimed: "the first 3 for you, the last 3 for me." The visitor played the first 3 confidently. He knew nothing of the fourth and less of the fifth that one took his bails, so he was around for the sixth. DAWSON kept that for gravy.

Memorial Match

Even at the close of his days DAWSON remained a giant. Residing for a short spell in St. Thomas he entered the league there and finished one season three years ago with combined batting and bowling honours. He planned his last game in August year and it is a bit ironical that this Tortolian who did so much to glorify Cricket in his native land played this time for St. Thomas against Tortola.

In honour of his name the Local Cricket Association plans a benefit match on Easter Monday, under the distinguished patronage of His Honour the Administrator. The general public is invited to attend and subscribe to a purse to be presented to his mother.

A hearty welcome is extended to ex-team mates and admirers in the neighbouring islands who may also feel inclined to subscribe to the memory of this glorious player.

FROM THE OBITUARY COLUMN OF THE APRIL 2, 1960 ISSUE OF THE "TORTOLA TIMES"

Deaths

Catherine Hodge of Free Bottom passed away on 19 March at the age of 79 years; on 24 March OWEN DAWSON of Road Town died at the age of 40 years, and on March 28 Samuel Freeman of Huntums Ghut passed on at the age of 82.

From "Cricket Notes" By Cyril Romney As Published In The April 23, 1960 Issue Of The "Tortola Times."

On Monday the annual event of a cricket match between married men and single men provided thrilling entertainment for a comparatively large crowd of cricket fans, the former maintaining the losing jinx of course. The game played this year in honour of the late OWEN DAWSON, was a benefit one and received quite a lot of publicity.

Strange but noteworthy personages watching the game included His Honour the Administrator and Mrs. Bryan, the Hon. J.O. Georges and Mrs. Georges, the Hon. H.R. Penn and Rev. Franklyn Roberts.

Contributions in favour of a purse for DAWSON's mother were received from players and spectators and the effort yielded $40. The Association is indeed grateful for the public response and chooses this medium of saying "THANKS" to all those who supported the cause financially and otherwise... "

"I am the batsman and the bat
I am the bowler and the ball
The umpire, the pavilion cat
The roller, pitch, and stumps and all"

Other outstanding cricketers of the BVI: – (no way complete)

Leando "Lando" Hamm	**Alexander "McGill" Titley**
Arthur Mathavious	Rupert Vanterpool
Basil Hodge	Ivan "Skipper" Evans
Ivan "Blinkey" Hodge	Ernest Todman
Robinson "Robbie" O'Neal	Denville O'Neal
Leopold Kendall	Edwin Prescott
Carlton Isaac	Maxwell Maduro
Carl "Carlie" Pickering	Alfredo "Mehorda" Niles
Alexander Ogilvie Shirley	Ira Maduro
Arnold "Hurlers" Smith	Larry McKelly
Aubrey Pickering	Charles Niles

Long ago, August Monday in Tortola meant the exciting CRICKET MATCH against the visiting ELEVEN. That was the drawing card – crowds came not to cheer the winning Queen, but the winning BVI ELEVEN.

Mario Connor, alias Black, son of May Flemming and James Connor was born in Road Town, Tortola on November 23, 1944. He was educated at the Road Town Primary School. After leaving school he worked in the construction field in Tortola and St. Thomas.

"Black" as he was known by his relatives, friends and fans was a renowned amateur softball player in the B.V.I. and the U.S.V.I.

Mario started playing softball at a very early age. He would take time out to play ball after school. As he matured, Mario would walk to Baugher's Bay every afternoon to play ball with the boys there. The very firstsoft ball club Mario played with was formed in Baugher's Bay.

Mario became famous when he formed the softball club known as the Astros. He pitched and batted very well. He was so outstanding that the fans graded him as a major league player. During some games home runs were hit one after the other. The home runs were hit so hard that it was said "he knocked "Momsel pot off the fire".

Learning about this outstanding play, the Manager for the Apache in St. Thomas came to Tortola and observed Mario playing on weekends. Mario was asked to pitch for the Apaches softball club in St. Thomas. This he did by ferrying to St. Thomas on game nights.

Later on, Mario resided in St. Thomas for many years and played for the Apaches. He also played in Tortola on weekends with his team the Astros.

Mario played with the B.V.I. National team although he was living in St. Thomas. It was while pitching for the B.V.I. National team on St. John in 1966 that Mario astounded the crowd by striking out 17 batters. His outstanding playing gave the B.V.I. National team the impetus to win the trophy presented that year.

Mario returned home in 1969. In spite of his injured leg, he trained many prominent softball players. He managed the Astros softball club until his untimely death August 14th, 1970.

Mario Connor

Laid to Rest: Was Outstanding Sports Figure

On Sunday (16th August) at 5:30 p.m. the body of Mario Connor, native son of Tortola, was laid to rest at the Methodist Cemetery in Road Town. More than twelve hundred mourners marched in the procession from the Hospital Mortuary to the burial site. The last rites at the grave side were conducted by Rev. John Whittle.

The deceased, age 26, was a popular sports figure who had earned the love and admiration of hundreds of fans on and off the ball field. He was also known and admired in the U.S. Virgin Islands where he also played softball and resided from time to time.

In the procession was a large turnout of ball players from Tortola. In uniforms of their respective teams, they marched in solemn cadence behind the hearse. The many ball teams in St. Thomas were also represented by the group of about fifteen ball players, managers and friends. By charter boat, they journeyed here to pay their last respects. Three of his buddies from that island along with others from Tortola, were pall bearers.

At the entrance to the cemetery, an arch was formed with two softball bats held by two of his buddies who were in their team uniform. The tribute was befitting as the deceased young man was known to have been a terrific batsman who on various occasions struck the ball clear out to the ball field, and on at least two occasions established a record distance.

Death came to the deceased on 14 August and was caused by a blood clot. He was at Peebles Hospital at the time undergoing treatment for an injured leg. He had expected to leave the Hospital in about two days. His death was a shock to the community.

The deceased is survived by his father, Mr. James Connor, four brothers Stanford, Milbourne, Edwy and Elmo; five sisters Eastlyn, Vivian, Vinie, Kirlin and Lita.

Memorial Address

By Carlos Downing Commissioner of the BVI Softball League, in commemoration of the late Owen Dawson and Mario Connor at the opening of the 1970-71 League at the Recreation ground on Sunday, 1st November.

ADDRESS

His Honour the Administrator; The Honourable Chief Minister Georges, relatives of the deceased Owen Dawson; Managers and Teams Assembled, Ladies and Gentlemen:

We are gathered here today on this familiar ground to formally open the 1970-71 B.V.I. Amateur Softball League and, firstly, to commemorate two softball players, both of Tortola, of outstanding qualities who departed this life at an early age and have left with us lasting memories.

OWEN DAWSON AND MARIO CONNOR who knew these grounds so well, are in spirit, here with today.

Owen Dawson is well known to many who are here. He was about 40 years of age at the time of his death. Everyone I have talked to expressed the view that Dawson was one of the best cricketers of these islands. He was, I understand, an all-rounder and a tremendous competitor on the field who was highly admired not only for his ability but also for good sportsmanship. He was in sports for many years.

Judging from the years Dawson was in flower, it may be taken for granted that cricket was his first love. But there is also information that with the advent of softball to Tortola, Dawson helped to popularize that sport and as a sportsman he became outstanding as a softball player also.

Our tribute to Owen Dawson today is relevant to the game we love, and we honour him for what he has done for softball and the sports on the whole.

What can we say of Mario Connor our friend and fellow softball player who died only recently in the springtime of life, and in whose honour we are also assembled on these grounds where he has played many a game.

We all miss Mario Connor ("Black" as he was known by his many friends). We miss him because he was a wonderful person and wonderful ballplayer. In fact, he was a shining star and one of the best examples for young men in sports to follow.

MARIO CONNOR loved softball. It was a great privilege to know this young man and to see him in action on the ball field. To say it in few words, since almost everyone knew him and his connection with softball, I will say that Mario Connor had everything and plenty to spare. He was big league material. As an example, we have seen him at bat on this same ballfield drive a pitch over the fence at right center, which is no small feat as every ballplayer here can testify. And he had done it more than once.

He was a great credit to softball in the British Virgin Islands as well as in St. Thomas, St. Croix and St. John where his extra-ordinary ability in that sport was also recognized.

It is said that to have friends one must be friendly. Mario Connor was that sort of person and he did, indeed, have many friends, including umpires.

We honour Mario Connor as the GREATEST SOFTBALL PLAYER the British Virgin Islands have produced and we also honour him in friendship.

As we go through the 1970-71 League it is the hope of the Association that the high examples of DAWSON and CONNOR will be followed, and there will be strong competition but with good sportsmanship.

THANK YOU

IRA MADURO - AN ACE CRICKETER

B.V.I. 1966 NATIONAL TEAM

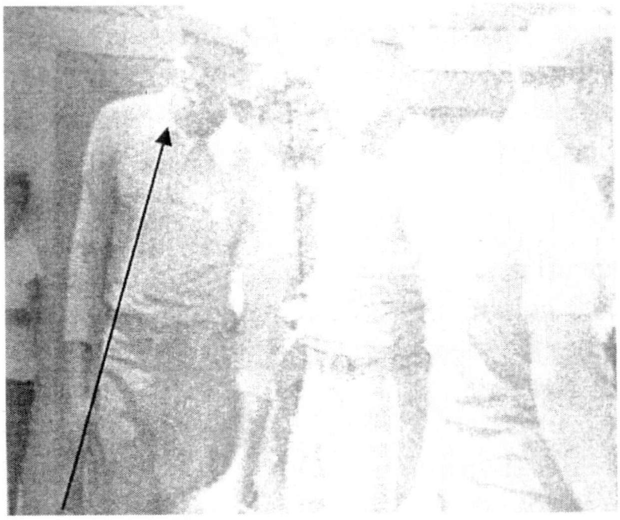

MARIO "BLACK" CONNOR - STRUCK BATTERS IN THE 1966 OVERSEAS TOURNAMENT

BVI 1966 NATIONAL TEAM

ARNOLD (CRACKERS) SMITH GETTING READY FOR THE GAME

CRICKETERS – A.O. SHIRLEY RECREATION GROUND 2005 ANGLICAN AND METHODIST CRICKETERS

"Titley's Tigers" about to leave for a softball match in St. John in the late 1950's. Pictured are in back left to right: Wendell Parsons, Capt of Govt. launch "St Ursula"

Gaston Penn and Mark Simmonds. Kneeling in front:

"THE PHYSICIAN HEALS, NATURE MAKES WELL"

— Aristotle

OUR DOCTORS, GRANNIES, NURSES, BONE SETTERS AND MASSAGERS

DOCTORS,

NURSES,

GRANNIES,

BONE SETTERS

AND

MASSAGERS

Dr. Reginald H. Georges

(FROM THE APRIL, 1943, ISSUE OF THE VIRGIN ISLANDS OFFICIAL BULLETIN)

During January of the year, an event of great historical importance to the British Virgin Islands took place. This event was the arrival of Dr. Reginald H. Georges, a native of Tortola, to be Junior Medical Officer in the B.V.I. for a short period.

Such an event had not occurred in over a century ago when John Lettsome, a native of Jost Van Dyke, BVI, returned to the Virgin Islands to practice medicine there, he being the same Dr. Lettsome who later achieved medical prominence in England... and was also the writer of the familiar lines:-

"John Lettsome,
Blisters, bleeds and sweats 'em'
If after any choose to die
I, John – lets 'em."

The arrival of Dr. Reginald Georges as a qualified medical officer thus marked an important milestone in the history of the B.V.I. for whereas Dr. Lettsome, though born in the British Virgin Islands was probably of European stock, Dr. Georges is entirely of native stock and his success cannot fail to be an inspiration to all native Virgin Islanders and a credit to his entire family and race. And now that he has gone to Antigua to be married and to practice medicine there for some time, we of the Virgin Islands extend to him our sincerest wishes for his continued success in all endeavours and for happiness in married life.

Dr. D.P. Wailling arrived in Tortola on August 15, 1927 and 15 years later he remembers his arrival. This is taken from the September, 1942 issue of the VIRGIN ISLANDS OFFICIAL BULLETIN.

Saturday, August 15 was the 15th anniversary of my first arrival in Tortola. Looking back, it does not seem so long. When I was selected as a candidate for the Leeward Islands Service, I had the privilege of meeting Mr. Edward Baynes the then Colonial Secretary who was on furlough in London, and it was he who saved me from being shipped to Jamaica by the Colonial Office. When the error was pointed out, passages were booked for Barbados which gave me an extra fortnight in which to prepare. Mr. Baynes expected me to be posted to Antigua and advised what I would require but I am glad I did not follow his advice about bringing a car.

To cut a long story short, we sailed from Avonmouth on the 18, July, 1927, on the Elders and Fyffes boat "SS CARARE" and had an exceedingly comfortable and pleasant trip across, reaching Barbados on the 31st. This good ship has, I believe since been sunk by enemy action, and I treasure as a memento a silver serviette ring which I won at deck tennis, and which I constantly use.

My posting orders were handed to me before I disembarked, but neither on board nor ashore was I able to learn anything about Tortola beyond that it was a small island up north which was constantly being destroyed by hurricanes. So much Igathered from Dr. Volume's letter, which said I would have a hurricane-proof house. We had to await the old "SS. DOMINICA" for 12 days and then started on our voyage up the islands: St. Lucia,

Guadeloupe, and then Antigua at 4 o'clock on the afternoon of the 13 August, the date from which my service counts.

That same night we reached St. Croix and started loading sugar; the whine of the winches made sleep impossible. The loading continued until 9 o'clock the next night, when we sailed for St. Thomas. I shall never forget the Manager's face when he had to open up to admit us to the "GRAND HOTEL" at 1:30 in the morning, and the added horror when I asked if we could have a cup of tea. I had been used to hotels out East, and now was I to know the rules of the West. However, a cup of tea then would have been most appreciated, but it was brusquely refused. Next morning, no early morning tea, nor any with breakfast, and then it dawned on me we were in an American territory where coffee is the national drink.

About 10 a.m. a tall, well set up, elderly man in uniform came up and introduced himself as Captain Titley of the Government launch "ST. URSULA", and after handing me a letter of welcome from the Commissioner, he informed me that we would be sailing at 1 o'clock. We had misgivings when we saw the tiny craft after the 4000 ton ships we had so far sailed on, but we were anxious to get to our new home and were assured it was only 34 miles.

Mr. Maduro, the engineer, and the deck hands, Joe and David, were introduced in turn, and Mrs. Marianetta Ham one of our fellow passengers "thanked God we had a fat doctor." Mr. Knight, the Seventh Day Adventist elder, and his wife, were among the company aboard. We had an indication of the kind of trip to expect, for no sooner had we got under way, than all the bundles were opened and basins and other less dignified utensils were produced. To us uninitiated, we thought our last day had come, and I was forced to exchange the seat of honour, a deck chair, for the security of a fixed bench.

The sea grew rather worse as we proceeded and Mrs. Knight tried to add words of comfort and cheer by telling us we were in St. James Passage, a place they called the Burial Ground, since so many boats were lost there. Our spirits were buoyed up when we felt we had reached Tortola, but soon crashed on being told there was another hour or more to go before we reached Road Town. However, when we did turn round the reef that opened up on Road Harbour, my wife and I felt it was worth waiting for, as to us it seemed the pick of all the islands we had seen and we fell in love with it right away.

Later when we were relating our experiences to the Commissioner, he laughed and said he had had the sea specially rolled out for us, and though at the time I thought it had been a pretty poor effort, when later I grew accustomed to the ways of the small boats I realized he was right; it would have been a calm trip for experienced sailors. I am glad St. Kitts now owns that tub, "ST. URSULA" and not us.

After we landed we went up to Government House at the invitation of the Commissioner, Mr. Clarkson, who was expecting a bachelor and was greatly surprised to see me with a wife and a daughter of four.

I had expressly asked the Colonial Secretary of Barbados to telegraph ahead, but this was never done. Mrs. Clarkson was away in England at the time, but we were made very happy at Government House and enjoyed a very pleasant week. It was still a greater joy to go into our own quarters after the other doctor had left and to open up our boxes and settle in.

On August 19 we received the information that Corporal J.N. Sheppard had been promoted to Sergeant as from 1st August. We congratulate Sergeant Sheppard, and hope that he will attain even greater promotion in the Force. The promotion naturally carries additional salary, and very welcome to a man with a family especially in these days; but money is not everything. I am sure there is even greater satisfaction in meriting a position of greater confidence and added responsibility, and I am sure Sergeant Sheppard will not fail this trust which has been placed in him. ...

MISS IRIS GEORGES, SENIOR NURSE, WILL TAKE CHARGE OF THE HOSPITAL DURING MISS EDWARDS' ABSENCE. LATER MISS GEORGES WAS MARRIED TO MR. ALLAN O'NEAL AND SERVED AS NURSE, MIDWIFE AND LOCAL PREACHER IN THE METHODIST CHURCHES OF THE BRITISH VIRGIN ISLANDS.

A tid-bit from 1942

"...For the latter half of August there have been no cigarettes in Town and I found the same state of affairs in Charlotte Amalie where Mr. Bruce is coming into his own, for his "SEA HORSE CIGARETTES" were everywhere in great demand.

Adina Looks Back

(By Sister Adina Donovan)

(From the Peebles Hospital Golden Jubilee Magazine – 1976)

We often take things so much for granted that we are sometimes shocked by the obvious. This happened to me when the 50th anniversary of the opening of the present hospital was being discussed. It suddenly dawned on me that for 35 years of my life, I had been involved with the institution in one way or another. And as I look back, it has been a hard but rewarding life in many ways.

My father died in 1925 and with a large family to support, my mother joined the nursing staff of the Cottage Hospital in Tortola. In those days with an English Matron and two local nurses it was almost a 24 hour a day job and as a little girl, in order to see my mother, I had to visit her since she had little time to spend with us. This was when I became aware of the hospital not as a place where the sick received attention, but as one that held people's mothers captive.

As a teenager, I joined the Rangers. Our leader was Mrs. Wailling, and her husband, who taught us first aid was Dr. D.P. Wailling, the longtime Medical Officer and Commissioner. I did exceptionally well in these classes which I enjoyed very much and I think that it was this that led me to consider nursing as a career. Dr. Wailling encouraged me but unfortunately there was no opening at the hospital. For a year or so I did voluntary work and assisted the doctor on his district rounds for which he gave me a small stipend from his own pocket.

I joined the staff as a student nurse on January 1, 1942. The English Matron of my earlier days had been replaced by a West Indian who served as Charge Nurse. Due to shortage of funds only a senior nurse and another student nurse completed the staff. There was then a five bed male ward, a five bed female ward and a single bed, private and space in the corridor and on the balcony for two more for emergency use. Two of us had day duty for about ten hours and one night duty for twelve. We had every other Sunday off after certain chores had been completed in the morning. Of course, if an emergency occurred all off-duty periods were cancelled. I can still see myself, scared out of my wits, with my hurricane lantern in hand, hurrying as fast as I could to get to Cockroach Hall to call the doctor for an emergency. Every dog in town must have known I was on my way and their barking did not help matters. And I often smile to myself when I think of trying to get the coal-pot burning to boil water for an emergency and the coals just would not catch. But those were the days when the town was dark and things were really rough.

In July 1944 I was transferred to Holberton Hospital in Antigua for training. I graduated after three years of general nursing and one of midwifery and at last was able to call myself a nurse.

In 1948 I returned home and was appointed Charge Nurse. The "Matron quarters" was turned into a maternity ward of six beds and a Nurse's Residence was built. The staff had increased to one senior nurse and five student nurses.

After 18 months I was sent for further training at the Royal College of Nursing in London for one year. I spent another 18 months at the hospital before I was seconded as a Ward Sister to the University Hospital of the West Indies in Jamaica.

I returned to Peebles Hospital as Nursing Sister in 1955. In 1960 the title of the post was again changed to become Chief Nursing Officer, a post I relinquished on my recent retirement from public service.

In my final stint, which covered just over 20 years, I saw the hospital grow from a cottage hospital, cramped, badly equipped and understaffed—to a small (38-bed) general hospital with an up-to-date operating theatre, X-ray and laboratory facilities, with a well trained staff of 10 nurses and 18 assistant nurses and an adequate medical staff. A number of local girls have gone both to the University Hospital of the West Indies and to various British hospitals for training. ... I do not think that anyone would argue about the benefit that the institution has been to the territory. Many people, doctors, nurses, administrators and private citizens have contributed to make this possible. Things have not always been rosy, times have often been hard, and while we have a long way to go, we have come a long way. ...

(Reprinted from "THE TORCH" September, 1948)

We also welcome back Miss M. Adina Donovan, who returned home in July, and assumed charge of the Hospital on August 1 .... We congratulate Sister Donovan on her achievements and wish her every success in her work... Miss Donovan's success is not only a personal triumph but also one for the Virgin Islands. Another native has been appointed to a position of responsibility. This we regard as a step in the right direction and it is generally conceded that such steps are few and far between.

Until people with a genuine interest in the islands and a keen desire to solve the multifarious problems which beset us, fill the senior posts in government service, no progress will be made, and up to the present there have been only a few non-indigenous officials who have evinced such an interest and desire. We must, therefore, support to the uttermost those of our own people who are able and willing to serve their community.

MAUDE CAROLINE DONOVAN née Maduro, was born in Road Town on September 11, 1887 to Samuel Maduro and his wife Anne. She attended St. George's School. She was married to Daniel Donovan on 21st September, 1904 and was the mother of five sons and four daughters.

Widowed in 1925, she joined the Cottage Hospital and began a nursing career in 1927 serving until 1935. On more than one occasion she was in charge of the Hospital between the appointments of Matrons. In 1940 she accepted an offer to serve as district nurse in Jost Van Dyke for two years, after which she did private nursing in the Road Town area and voluntary work at the Cottage Hospital. She was popularly and affectionately known as Nurse D. She died at her home in Road Town on 20 June, 1963.

ETHELFREDA PICKERING TITLEY, joined the staff at Peebles Hospital in 1933 as an untrained nurse, some six years after the Hospital was founded. This move was prompted not by the monetary attraction of the post—for the salary was then only 39 per month—nor for the work hours, because the shifts were very lengthy. Nurses at that time worked two shifts, of twelve hours each. They were on night duty for two weeks, then for two weeks during the daytime with a mere one day off every two weeks. Rather, her move was prompted by a desire to help as evidenced by the many voluntary hours during which she attended the hospital before she was actually employed there. Despite the conditions, Mrs. Titley enjoyed her work, especially that of assisting in theatre and with midwifery and considered the experience worthwhile. Mrs. Titley remembers working with Dr. Wailling, the only doctor on the island at the time and one time Acting Commissioner.

MARY DAVIES was born to Osmond and Mary Louisa Davies of East End on October 25, 1890. She received her early education at the Primary School at East End. Miss Davies became known throughout the British Virgin Islands for her skill as a midwife. For 37 years she served the Territory in that capacity, delivering her last baby two months before she passed away on July 3, 1965. For such meritorious service she was awarded BEM in 1957 by HER MAJESTY QUEEN ELIZABETH II. The following is an extract from the Speech made by the then Commissioner about Miss M.L. Davies on June 13, 1957. Miss Davies had delivered 600 babies by the time she ceased practicing.

"Miss Davies was first employed by Government in 1926 as a student nurse at the Cottage Hospital. She was sent to Antigua for training early in 1929 and returned to Tortola late in 1930 after completing her midwifery course. On her return to Tortola, she was not immediately re-employed by Government and went into private practice as a midwife. She was recalled to the service in 1931 but resigned her appointment as a midwife, and has successfully delivered some 700 cases. Miss Davies filled a real need in this Colony as a private midwife and was at one time, for many years, the only qualified midwife in private practice. She has always been willing to nurse the sick even if they could not meet her modest charge and in this way eased the burden that would have been placed on the inadequate hospital services existing in these islands until recently."

DOLORITA HENDRICKS – nee Hatchett, daughter of Mr. & Mrs. Hatchett of Great Harbour, Jost Van Dyke, traveled to Tortola in 1940 to begin her nursing career at the Hospital which was then a cottage, where she met in charge nurse, Iris Edwards. Her co-workers were Iris O'Neal nee George, Sylvia Knight and Adina Donovan. After three years she returned to Jost Van Dyke and was in charge of the district there. For over a quarter of a century she gave devoted and loyal service to the people of that island. She travelled mainly on foot; she performed her duties and remained in the service until her death in 1969. Her daughter who followed in her footsteps was appointed District Nurse on Jost Van Dyke in 1970.

Midwives and "The Grannies"

The midwives being honoured are the representatives of that group of valiant compassionate women, "The Grannies", who in addition to rearing large families of their own, took on the additional task of rendering bedside care to women during childbirth. Their formal training was primarily in the school of their own experience as mothers. They also had knowledge of folk medicine and practice experience on the job, initially under the watchful eye of an elderly midwife, who was about to retire.

They received little or no remuneration ... nevertheless they were able to maintain a system of primary health care ... the midwives were the true and principal custodians of the community's health prior to and even after 1921. The community is indeed indebted to them for the role they have played in the evolution of our Health System. (Rita Frett Georges in "A Tribute to District Midwives)

ANEGADA

Angelina Varlack
Camella Wells
Mary White
Leslie Potter
Francis Vanterpool
Agnes Smith

EAST END/LONG LOOK

Martha Dawson
Rosamund Malone
Celestine Thomas
Mary Magdalene Thomas Rabsatt (Micy)
Rosalind Penn

BELLE VUE/COOTEN BAY/FAHIE-HILL

Christiana Freeman

Catherine Parrott "Katie Ben". Katie served the Belle Vue, Cooten Bay, Long Trench, Fahie Hill areas for many years in the 1920's to the early 1940's. In addition to the women of the area, she was the "granny" who brought her daughters and granddaughters 'to bed' at the time of their 'lying in'. She was born in 1874 to Francis "Fannie Ben" and Benjamin Hetherington. At the time of her death on April 19th 1945 at the age of 71, she had acted as 'granny' at the birth of over 70 plus grandchildren, which included several sets of twins, and great grandchildren. It seems as "Katie" learned this skill from her mother who was also a midwife for that area.

BREWERS BAY

Manuelita Christopher

VIRGIN GORDA

Trephina George
Adria Sprauve
Esther O'Neal
Iris Georges O'Neal

SOLDIER'S HILL

Sylvanita Rhymer

WEST END/CARROT BAY/LITTLE APPLE BAY

Elizabeth Donovan "Betty Blue"
Elizabeth Leonard "Mama Betty"
Christiana Smith "Shana"
Teresa Blyden "Friend Dolie"
Juliana Callwood "Lady"
Ann Dawson "Lilantie"

Bone Setters and Massagers

Once upon a time there was one doctor in the B.V.I. We should say only a quarter of a doctor, because the doctor also served as Commissioner or (head of the Government), Magistrate, and Treasurer. There was no orthopaedist, but the Territory was fortunate to have a number of men and women who had somehow learned to diagnose joint dislocations and had become expert at the art of bone settings.

When a person suffered a fall or developed any condition causing severe pain in the area of a joint, off he went to the nearest setter who would put him through the painful exercise of the massage and setting. Sometimes the patient could hear the "click" as the dislocated bone returned to its socket.

Famous bone setters such as ROSA MALONE have been known to cure patients who obtained no relief from medical treatment in the hospital.

There were others such as:

Catherine Lettsome
Ronald Lettsome
Ishmael Fahie
Juliana Callwood
Joe Leonard
Samuel Percival
Caroline Henley
Rosa Penn
Marie Todman of the Hope
Alberta Frett

Sonny Lettsome
Rosamond Malone
Elizabeth Donovan
Marcy Leonard
Esmie Dawson
Mena Henley Leonard
Freddie Williams
Eynah Todman
Celestine Thomas
Isaac "Beauty" Thomas

Modern people laugh at the idea of unlearned persons being possessed of such skill, but they did it, their treatment worked and many persons can testify to the skill of the local bone setters.

2004 – Several massage parlours have been opened in the territory and chiropractors have become popular.

Dentists

Mr. F.C. Ward (U.K)
Mrs. B. Brodie (Belgium)

Cupping and Leeching

There were many methods used to relieve aches and pains in the old days. One of these was called "cupping". From the information received the following was the method used to "cup" a blow that caused a bruise, thus causing blood to congeal under the skin.

The patient was taken to someone who was an expert in the art of "Cupping." A small calabash "gobie" was prepared by cutting a very small hole, the size of a "bululoo" (2 cents piece, about the size of today's half dollar) in the end of the gobie. The inside of the "gobie" was then dampened with cane rum. (Cane rum is very flammable)

The damaged area of the body was given a small "gash" (cut) with a razor blade that was used for no other purpose than to cut bruised areas. The "cup" was then lit with a match held directly over the bruised area where the cut was made. The rum and flame caused a suction which held the "cup" in place.

The suction drew the "bruised blood" from the injured area and this suction continued until all the blood congested in the area was removed. The "cup" then fell off its own accord, the suction now being released.

Another method of removing "bruised blood" was by the use of a leech, an insect similar in looks to the caterpillar. This leech or worm would pierce the injured area and draw out the blood.

It, too, would fall off when the area was free from congestion. Again this method like the one above was only applied by persons well versed in this art.

It is believed that cupping was a medical form used in Africa and was also brought to the Territory by persons who saw it applied in Santo Domingo. The leech method seems also to have been brought in from Santo Domingo but it seems that it was also known to persons here before our men ventured to Santo Domingo.

From information received the following persons were well versed in the art of "CUPPING" and applying "LEECHES"

CUPPING:	Mrs. Jane Eliza Henley
LEECHES:	Mrs. Caroline "Tonco" Henley Mrs. Louisan Gibbs Penn

The Past – Cottage Hospital

Diagram of the Peebles Hospital

The Present – Peebles Hospital

SECOND PLACE LOGO

The Whips are for slavery. Black semi-circle for the darkness. Candle was the source of light in the past and the bulb is the present. VIGILATE is today and the broken whips show freedom and advancement in Technology.

Submitted by: JACQUELINE NIBBS
FORM II
B.VI. High School

"Mid pleasures and palaces
Though we may roam
Be it ever so humble
There's no place like home"

"Home, Sweet Home – J. Howard Payne

SALTS

OF

THE

EARTH

MRS. MATHILDA HODGE-RONAN (NEN YA-YA) OF WEST END

MS. MELVINA HODGE OF WEST END

WHERE WOULD WE BE WITHOUT THESE STALWARTS?

CLAREMOND FLOYD DAVIES

the only person of East End who rendered service in all The Virgin Islands

ROSANNA HELENA SMITH

"Her soul doth magnify the Lord
And her spirit hath rejoiced in God her Saviour"

ROSANNA HELENA SMITH was born on November 22, 1890. Together with her husband, the late HENRY SMITH of Soldier's Hill, she raised a large family of 13 children — 7 daughters and 6 sons, 9 of whom are still alive.

Mrs. Smith developed a love for singing from a very early age and joined the band of carolers known as "GREAT BRITAIN UNITY BAND", the leadership of which she took over from the late CALELITA GREAVES in 1924. Every year for 60 years Mrs. Smith had taken the good tidings of Christmas to neighbours and friends all over Tortola—trudging over the watery and muddy roads and braving the chilly weather typical at Christmas time. And every year people look forward to the visit of GREAT BRITAIN. It would not seem like Christmas without them and their colourful banner and flag.

The name "GREAT BRITAIN UNITY BAN" leads one to think of patriotism and the days when everyone sang "Rule Britannia." On Christmas morning when the bands confronted each other and the competition was really stiff, it took the strong and courageous leadership of our sister to maintain order while GREAT BRITAIN UNITY BAND went home really feeling that they ruled the waves of carolers. To have raised such a large family and command the respect and admiration of her followers for 60 years is an indication of the moral and physical strength which our sister possesses.

When Mother's Day was celebrated and in referring to some women of the Bible one preacher reminded us that there are a number of women about whom little is said or known, yet if we stopped to read the little that has been said, we find that they were great women indeed. I believe that the same can be said of MRS. ROSANNA HELENA SMITH. She has been a member of this Church for many years and still attends. I can recall having attended rehearsals of GREAT BRITAIN UNITY BAND many years ago. Without fail the evening's proceedings always began with the song, "In the Church of God..." and this was followed by the passage from Matthew, "Now when Jesus was born..." In her simple but meaningful way our sister has been preaching the gospel.

She has done, and continues to do, what she can, is to me a fitting description for our Sister ROSANNA HELENA SMITH. During this year when we celebrate our 150th Anniversary Emancipation from slavery, I think it most fitting that the part which she played in keeping alive this aspect of our culture should be recognized.

Submitted by Mrs. Doris Braithwaite
Methodist Circuit Steward

Mr. Emile Smith of Long Trench "BRUDDA EMILE" on His mule. His brand of humour is as rare as his transportation.

DIPPING VAT

Cattle going in and out used to be a common sight.

A jack of all trades.

Catherine Potter Lettsome A Centenarian

Christopher Fleming (1851-1935)

Christopher Fleming is one of the names that still has the power to make some of the older generation shake their heads knowingly and say "That was a man." Fleming was born in the year 1851 in the Long Look area of Tortola and was apparently a jack-of-all-trades since people will tell you that he was a sailor, a mason and a registrar. But whatever else he did, one thing is certain—that he was a prominent citizen of his day.

Fleming was married to Victoria Penn who gave him several children—five of whom are still alive. Four live on St. John, U.S. Virgin Islands and one in the Long Look district of Tortola.

From all accounts he held lectures in the area and spoke on any important decision that had to be made by government. One lady remarks—"That man was a brilliant man. He was really very intelligent, and his handwriting, it was beautiful." His services were in demand quite often, not only to sign documents but also to write letters for a number of his illiterate friends and associates.

As a sailor, Fleming must have done his share of smuggling which may be described as a way of life at that time. It is probably as a result of one of the less fortunate attempts at smuggling that he is best remembered.

Late in the 19th century, a boat belonging to a group of men from Long Look was seized. Fleming and a number of other men from the area—including persons like Joe Skelton, Tommy Pickering, Nelson Dawson, Joseph Peter Gordon, James Osmond Thomas (Bim) and James Thomas (Boodoo)—armed themselves with cutlasses and guns and soon presented themselves to the President—the title was later changed to Commissioner—in Road Town demanding the release of the boat. On seeing the armed men Mr. Edward James Cameron, the President at that time, panicked and ran from his office.[1]

He lost little time in summoning help. He appealed to the authorities in St. Thomas and within a few days some Danish soldiers arrived on the island but could do very little to help. Eventually Fleming and the other men were rounded up and sent to Antigua for trial. Both Fleming and Pickering were sentenced to six months in jail while the others returned home. The gun used by Fleming may be seen today in "O'NEAL'S MUSEUM" in Road T[2]own.

(STRAIGHT FROM US VOL. I)

Henry "Tampo" Fahie

HENRY "TAMPOO" FAHIE, stood over 6 feet tall and came from the area of Tortola known as Manchester in the BelleVue section of the territory. He was one of the sons of JAMES and LUCRETIA FAHIE. His strength was as of "the strength of ten" and at prayer meetings at the Wesleyville (Bellevue) Church when he got the "spirit" no one took the chance to hold him. Carried by his faith in the "spirit" his strength seemed to increase and he was known to toss men about as if they were bits of paper. The following poem is taken from the book of poems entitled "REFLECTIONS" published in 1967 by St. Thomian, CORNELIUS L. EMANUEL.

THE LEGEND OF TAMPOO

Now Tampoo was the strongest man
In all the Virgin Isles
His teeth could lift one hundred pounds
And carry it for miles.

Some rumor had it that an ass
Annoyed him with its bray;
He slapped that donkey on the head
And put the beast away!

Before you knew these rumors flew
And reached the ears of Dully
A champion boxer in his right
Who couldn't stand a bully.

He went forthwith to German Wharf (*)
Swearing a hundred oaths;
Where Tampoo singlehandedly
Raised cows from British boats.

He challenged him to combat then
To prove the stronger man;
The only thing that Tampoo said;
"Ah wan' to ketch he one."

They fought all day and half that night;
It was no sight to leave;
With Dully's fancy footwork, jabs,
Right-cross, and bob-and-weave!
Great Tampoo swung his mighty arms
(He couldn't see the man!)
And grunted in frustrated rage:

"Ah wan' to ketch he one."

Now Dully's punches missed their mark
So far away was he;
But seeing Tampoo turn around
Came in adventurously –
And just the breeze from Tampoo's hand
Knocked Dully in the sea!

So Dully, with three broken ribs
And Tampoo still is muttering; "
Ah didn't ketch he one."

* German wharf—Now West Indian Company Docks

The Shark Company

The Shark Company Through the Eyes of A Youngster

This is the way sharks were caught in the early years of the twenties. We at that time used a 1/4 inch rope with a large galvanized hook. Bait was a small fish or a large piece of meat. We used a large floating object set out mostly in the evening. Early next morning we would go in search of the catch. Sometimes one person had at least five to six traps, and sometimes the catch used to be between two or three sharks which brought the total per day to about twelve to fifteen sharks small and large.

But one day a special shark was caught two miles west of Guana Island. This one was towed in behind the boat. On its arrival a large crowd gathered to see this great shark. The scale that was on site was 1500 pounds (could handle 1500 pounds). This special shark carried the scale right down to the limit, which means that this shark was more than 1500 pounds.

This is what I can remember. I was about five or six years old then. I hope my account will throw some light on your story.

Obel Penn, East End

Grandma Marie Speaks to Leon-The Shark Company

Catching sharks for a profit, was the title of an article in The B.V. Islander, January 1974 (p.41). What was hoped for in that article had already taken place in East End, Tortola in the 1920's where SHARK COMPANY was established in the area where the East End Clinic (Iris Penn-Smith Marie Durante-Wheatley. One of the coppers used in the boiling process was saved by my grandmother. Marie Durante-Wheatley. It now sits in my parents' garden.

The manager/owner of the Shark Company, James Young, told the people of East End that the owned by the Wheatley's (James Young) was named after his great grandfather. Some years later, after the company no longer existed, Mr. Young gave my grandmother an exercise book that became the envy of the village. The pages did not blot when the stick pen of that times was used. On the cover of the book were traffic signs and how to walk in traffic. While this information was not useful in East End at the time because there were no vehicles, the book was prized possession that every teacher had to touch and examine and every student wished they were as lucky as Marie Durante.

The Shark Company

According to my grandmother, the manufacturing process included the making of oil from the liver of the shark and jewellery from the teeth. Since shark meat was not a delicacy in those days, the flesh was probab;y used as additional bait.

The factory was a wooden building with a galvanized roof. This housed some of the activities while some activities took place on a large barge anchored in the immediate area. Once fishermen brought in the catch which was killed on the large barge and liver taken out, the boiling process began. Large pans filled with liver were hung from a wire into the boiling water beneath and the oil was actually steamed out of the liver. The oil was poured into other containers to be transported to St. Thomas in the Company's smaller boat, the Venus. This boat took the oil to the Red Hook area of St. Thomas from where it was sent to other places. Perhaps, it was further refined or merely transshipped.

Belts were made from the skin of the shark and ornaments like earrings and bracelets were made from the teeth. My grandmother remembers the teeth being strung on silver wire to make the ornaments.

The Shark Company must have put much needed money in the hands of local fisherman, and kept some men at home instead off to Santo Domingo to work in the sugar cane fields.

Tell me more Grandmother!

Leon Wheatley

THE WOODEN AND "TRASH" HOUSE BUILDERS

WELL PRESERVED LOVELY OLD HOMES AT
ROAD TOWN
AND CANE GARDEN BAY

UNUSUAL ARCHITECTURE
ZION HILL METHODIST CHURCH AT WEST END
THE BAND STAND AT ROAD TOWN

Donated by the children of Mr. Clarence Christian

I remember, I remember
The house where I was born
The little window where the sun
Came peeping in at morn.

Up until the immediate post World War II period, the villages of the British Virgin Islands consisted of many thatch "trash" houses. These were not status symbols as in the United Kingdom. They represented Virgin Islander's effort at restoration after two devastating hurricanes of 1916 and 1924. Most often the walls of the house were made of wood, but in some communities, Carrot Bay for example, they were made of "wattle and daub". The roof was thatched by one of the local thatchers. Some names which come to mind—not limited to these alone—are as follows:

Benjamin Brathwaite "Pinchie"	Todman's Estate
Theophilus Purcell "Toppie"	Diamond Estate
Adrian Todman	Georges Northside
Edward "Hoyt" Todman	Joe's Hill
Benjamin Brathwaite "Aughtful"	Leonards
Archie Adams	Chalwell Estate
William "Willie" Niles	Road Town
Jose Donovan	Carrot Bay
John James Donovan	Carrot Bay
Sandy Donovan	Carrot Bay
"Jen" Brewley	Baughers Bay
Isaac Williams	Carrot Bay
Isaac Cameron	Cappoons Bay
Marcy Leonard	Carrot Bay
Ezekiel Thomas	Cappoons Bay
Elick Cameron	Cappoons Bay

They used a special sewing needle which they made from wood and "cat's claw" withes for thread. Although the thatching was not nearly as pleasing to the eye as that done in the U.K. it did however display some artistic talent.

The roof was first lined with rods which had been cut from trees and scraped to remove the brown bark, and coconut leaves from which the central had been removed. Finally, the "thatch" - bundles of redhead grass which had been cut and dried was applied by use of the needle and thread.

Of course, there were the house builders or carpenters, who constructed the wooden walls and floors of the thatched house. They also built wooden houses with galvanized roofing - called "Silvertops" in some areas of the country. A few of these homes are still in existence today. In some cases the roofs were covered with asphalt locally called "Felt", but these houses have disappeared.

In the good old days there were no rules governing the building industry. Accordingly, no architectural drawings were made and no regulation by a Land Development Control Authority and Building Authority as is normal today.

A person wishing to construct a house simply asked a "carpenter" as a builder was called locally to do the job. Of course, he was told what size house was wanted and how many rooms. It was often believed that the more doors there were to the house the more attractive it looked, and a carpenter was recognized by the "pitch" he gave to the roof of the house he built. Some of the past carpenters - not limited were:

EAST END:

William Stoutt
Joseph Gordon
Richard Stoutt

WEST END:

Wally Smith
Daniel Smith
Stanley Smith
Rudolph Smith

ROAD TOWN AND ENVIRONS:

Osmond Roach
James "Jimmie" Shirley
Denniel Turnbull
Anthon Forbes
Allan Harrigan
Alexander Turnbull
Alfred "Todo" Freeman
Elvin Hodge
Randolph Dawson
William Roach*
Evan Evans
Rudolph Jennings
David Freeman
Evelyn Hodge
Archibald Abednego
Rupert Vanterpool
Osmond Brathwaite

CARROT BAY/CAPPOONS BAY/LITTLE APPLE BAY

Stanley Smith
Osmond Donovan
Edmund Romney
King Arthur Donovan
Alfred Cameron
Abraham Leonard

* Also made the box oven which was the first popular indoor/outdoor oven. See Coals of Fire by Verna P. Moll.

LIMPING JACK'S THATCH (TRASH) HOUSE

MT. HEALTHY SUGAR MILL RESTORED BY REGINALD CALLWOOD OF LONG TRENCH AND ST. JOHN

THE DUNGEON AT SEA COWS BAY – THERE WAS WEEPING AND WAILING

THE REMAINS OF THORNTON HOUSE AT PLEASANT VALLEY. BELIEVE IT OR NOT THE WASHINGTON CAPITOL WAS DESIGNED HERE

RIGHTEOUS CHURCH GOERS AND UNRIGHTEOUS SCHOOL CHILDREN WERE ALL PART OF THIS SCENE --- AT EAST END METHODIST CHURCH

THIS SITE MARKS THE
B. V. I.
FIRST METHODIST BUILDING
ERECTED 5 NOV. 1810
REBUILT 1846, 1869, 1875

"there was an old hen
and she had a wooden leg
and every damned morning
she laid another egg
she was the best damned chicken
on the whole damned farm
and another little drink
wouldn't do any harm"

American Folksong

OUR

DISTILLERS

AND

THEIR

WORKS"

PICKERING'S DISTILLERY AT BAUGHERS BAY (near present PWD)

MULE LOUIE POWER
"LOUIE LOOSE YO MULE"

The Sugar Industry in Tortola

The sugar plantation was one of the most dramatic sights in the West Indies. It was also the core of the economy during the early centuries. The flat swampy areas contributed to much of its success. The Virgin Islands though, had limited and meager lands since they are mountainous in the interior and the swamps around the seashore are too salty for the proper growth of sugar cane. ...Today there are several ruins of sugar 'estates', some of them being only tourist sights. Only two estates were left producing cane rum on a small scale. These were owned by Mr. Owen "Owie" Callwood of Cane Garden Bay. The factory at Baugher's Bay had ceased operations but Mr. Callwood's factory which is situated on the western coast of Tortola and partly hidden by huge breadfruit trees is still in operation.

Today, his cane rum carries the name "Arundel". Mr. Callwood succeeded his father who taught him the trade some 70 years ago when the younger Callwood was but a boy. Today, he grows his own sugar cane as well as he receives sugar canes from farmers on other parts of the islands. ...The fresh juice is boiled a little then poured into barrels. An acid is added to this juice and it is left to ferment. At this stage it is called "mash". This "mash" is taken to the distillery through pipes and poured into "stills" for boiling.

The vapour passes through huge multi-joined copper pipes and spirals down to a pipe line which is suspended into a cistern filled with cold water. Here it condenses and trickles out, a cool colourless fluid with a strong smell.

Mr. Callwood explained that the first rum from each batch is the strongest, up to 80% proof but it gets weaker as the batch finishes. The rum is poured into barrels to cool, cure and store, then it is transferred into demijohns and shipped...

Mr. Pickering who used to be the proprietor of the distillery at Baugher's Bay once hinted that the job was not as easy as it seemed. He said he wanted to carry on the industry but no one wanted to plant sugar cane anymore. That was when he abandoned the idea and produced small amounts of cane rum from the sugar cane grown on the factory grounds. This rum was sold to local bars.

Old farmers might long for the industry to be brought alive again since it was also a time for spreeing. At "crop over" which happened twice a year, all workers got together on the factory grounds where they cooked, ate, drank and sometimes danced to the music of the scratch band. The sound of conch shells signalled the last sugar cane being pushed through the grinders. This drew everyonr nearby to eat, drink, and boast about about the success of the crop. Some of our well-known distillers were:

The Callwood family of Cane Garden Bay
Ernest Jacobs
Howie Scatliffe
Morris Parsons
Mr. Warner
Ernest Pickering
Ernest Parsons
Samuel Sammy Freeman
Samuel Sammy Parsons

Distilleries were located at Baughers Bay, Cane Garden Bay, Brewers Bay, and Georges Northside. (Excerpts for the SUGAR INDUSTRY taken from "EDUCATION WEEK 1984 published by the Education Department)

CALLWOOD'S DISTILLERY AT CANE GARDEN BAY. THE CANE RUM STILL KILLS "WORMS" AND "GAS"

"THE NEARER THE BONE THE SWEETER THE MEAT"

SPECIAL

FOODS

AND

BEVERAGES

RECIPES

"Be present at our table Lord,
Be here and everywhere adored
These creatures bless and grant that we,
May feast in paradise with thee" Amen.
Said at "make lunch" in Methodist schools

TANNIA SOUP

1/2 lb salt beef or pigtail
1-1/2lbs. tannia quartered
1 small onion sliced or chopped
1 sprig of thyme
dumplings (droppers)
sugar (if desired)
1 blade chive
1 small tomato chopped
2 quarts water
1 cup milk
1 cup milk
salt & pepper to taste

Wash meat with lime and boil in 2 quarts water. Add seasonings and simmer until meat is tender. Season with salt and pepper to taste. Add tannias and dumplings. Cook until tannias are soft and dumplings float to top. Add milk and cook for another 3-5 minutes. Remove from heat and sweeten to taste. Serve hot. Serve 6 persons.

MAN SOUP

This dish was probably name because it originated with farmers who prepared their own lunches on the job (in the fields, plantation or ground as they were popularly called)

1-1/2 lbs sweet potato quartered
1/2 lb yam
2 blades chives
2 tbs cream or 1 tbs margarine
1 tomato
1 slice pumpkin
salt & pepper to taste
dumplings (optional)
1-1/2 lbs tannia quartered
1/2 lb pigtail or pigmouth
1 pt milk
1 sprig thyme
few cabbage leaves or okra
3 qts. water
sugar (optional)

Clean and boil pignout with chives and thyme in 3 quarts water. When the meat is tender add cut up cabbage leaves, peeled tannias, potatoes, yam and pumpkin. Add dumplings and simmer until ground provisions are soft and dumplings float to top. Add salt and pepper to taste. Add milk, stirring occasionally. Remove from heat. Add sugar to taste. Serve hot.

SWEET POTATO PUDDING

2 lbs sweet potato
1 tannia
1/4 pumpkin
1/2 c flour
1 c. grated coconut
2 oz melted fat
1/2 c sugar
1/2 tsp nutmeg
1/2 tsp cinnamon
salt and pepper to taste
1 c milk or hot water

Wash and peel provisions. Grate sweet potato, pumpkin and tannia. Mix grated coconut, sugar, melted fat and hot water or milk together and pour over potato mixture. Add remaining ingredients until a knife inserted comes out clean.

CASSAVA BREAD

3 lbs cassava - about 6 c. meal1
3 tsp. salt2

Peel and wash cassava. Dry and grate very fine. Wring out all the juice using a clean strong muslin cloth. Sift the meal and spread out to dry. Add salt. Heat a baking iron or "tawa" oven to moderate heat. Spread about 2 cups meal inside the iron ring. Flatten and press the bread into shape with a knife of palette. Turn over when slightly brown. Remove from "tawa" and put in the sun until the bread ends are quite dry and stif[3]f.

DUCKNOR

1 - 1 1/2 cups grated green corn
3/4 c. sugar (or to taste)
1/2 tsp. spice
1/2 c. flour
banana leaves
1 small coconut - grated
4 tb. melted margarine
1/2 tsp. nutmeg
milk to mix
salt and pepper to taste

Mix together all ingredients, adding the milk last to make a batter of dropping consistency. Season to taste. Pour about 2 tablespoons of mixture on a piece of steamed or quailed banana leaf and tie securely. Put in boiling water and cook for 30 minutes or until firm.

COCONUT BREAD

2 c. coconut
1 tsp salt
3/4 c sugar
1/2 tsp nutmeg
1/2 tsp cinnamon
milk of water to mix to a stiff dough
4 c flour
2 eggs beaten
3 tsp baking power
1 tsp. vanilla essence
2/3 c. shortening

Sift flour, salt and baking power together. Add spices, coconut and sugar. Melt shortening and add to beaten eggs. Add to flour mixture. Add flavoring and enough water or milk to make a stiff but pliable dough. Knead on a floured board. Shape and bake in greased tins in a moderate oven 350 degrees. F. until brown.

OKRA FUNGI

4 okras, washed and cut up
1 tsp. salt
1 tbs margarine
2 – ½ c boiling water
1 – ¼ c. cornmeal

Boil cut up okras in water. To rapidly boiling water add salt. Sprinkle cornmeal in slowly. Allow water to boil over cornmeal stir briskly to prevent lumping. When well mixed add margarine. Cover and steam for about 5 minutes stirring occasionally. Serve hot.

CORNMEAL PAP

1 c milk — cow's milk
1 stick cinnamon
¼ c. sugar
1 tsp. margarine
1 c. boiling water
1 c. cornmeal
1 tsp. salt

Bring to a boil milk, water, salt and cinnamon. Add cornmeal stirring constantly to prevent lumping. Add sugar and butter and continue stirring until mixture begins to thicken. Lower heat, and cook for 10-15 minutes, stirring occasionally. Serve with raisins if so desired.

SALTFISH AND RICE

1 lb saltfish
1 c. tomatoes (canned)
1 sprig thyme
1 clove garlic—chopped
3 c. boiling water
1/2 c. shortening
1 sprig parsley
1 tbs chopped green pepper
2 c. rice
1 med. onion

Soak fish, remove bones and skin. Saute onion, tomatoes, green pepper, thyme, garlic in shortening. Pick saltfish in fine pieces, add shortening and allow to sauté. Add boiling water and boil rapidly before adding rice. Slowly cook uncovered until water disappears. Cover and steam until grains are tender.

NATIVE SEASONING

1 c. rock salt, pounded
4 tsp black pepper
1\2 tsp cloves
1 sprig celery
1 sprig parsley
1 tsp mace
1 tsp nutmeg
5 cloves garlic

Combine all ingredients by putting in a mortar and pounding with a pestle until well mixed. Store in a jar for future use. This seasoning is used to flavor all types' meat, fish, chicken, turkey. Hot red pepper may be used instead of black pepper.

BOILED CONCHS IN BUTTER SAUCE

4-5 lbs. conch
2-3 lbs. margarine
2-3 tsp cooking oil
1/2 c. water
1 med onion, sliced
Juice of 1 lime
hot pepper (optional)
salt to taste

Boil conchs until tender. Drain and cut into small pieces. Cook sliced onion in 1/2 c. water until tender. Add margarine, cooking oil, hot pepper to taste and boil slowly for about 5 minutes. Add conchs to sauce. Season to taste with salt and cook a few minutes longer.

BOIL FISH BAUGHERS BAY BAYSIDE STYLE

Fish—cleaned and seasoned. Use either native seasoning or Salt Island salt and black pepper to taste.

Place fish on aluminum foil and baste with lots of margarine. Make sure to stuff margarine in belly and gashes. Cover fish with sliced onions. Roll fish, onions in foil. Place on hot galvanize over an outdoor fire.

To really get the best form this dish, it must be cooked at the seaside, with the galvanize being placed over 3 rockstone fireplace. Allow to broil about 20-25 minutes or until done. The best fish to use it seems are pot fish although other fish may be used.

On any given Saturday morning this is the dish that is being prepared by the boys of the "Bayside Bar in Baughers Bay and lucky the passerby who is asked to partake of this delicacy...

SUGARCANE WINE

6 pieces, joints of sugarcane
6-8 pts water
1 lb raisins
2 pieces spice
1 tsp yeast
1 piece ginger
sugar to taste

Cut sugar cane into very small pieces. Sweeten the water and add to sugar cane. Add spice and ginger. Let stand for 14 days. Strain and add yeast and raisins. Strain and bottle after 3-4 weeks.

SOURSOP DRINK

1 large ripe soursop
1 -1/2 c sugar
4 cups hot water
½ c. evaporated milk

Wash and peel soursop. Add ½ the hot water to the soursop and mask to a pulp. Strain through a colander. Add the rest of the hot water and strain. Add sugar to the soursop juice sweeten and add milk. Mix well. Chill and serve.

BOILED SUGAR APPLE

Boiled sugar apple is unique to the British Virgin Islands. The sugar apple is peeled and the centre core or plug removed. It is placed in boiling salted water. It is boiled until a knife can pass through easily and immediately removed from the water. The texture is similar to yam and some folks refer to it as seedy yam. Sugar apple goes well with boiled fish, corned pork and pig tail.

FLOUR WOULD HAVE BEEN KNEADED ON A TABLE SUCH AS THIS IN THE PROCESS OF MAKING BREAD OR DUMPLINGS

MISS EDNA AT THE OVEN IN HER YARD AT CANE GARDEN BAY

TART MAKING – THE VIRGIN ISLAND WAY

Tart dough is short curst pastry.

Typical Recipe

1 cup Sugar (white, brown or mixed)
1/2 cup Crisco
1/2 cup Margarine or butter (pot spoon size)
1 Egg
1/2 cup Milk or water
3 teaspoons Baking powder
1 tsp. Vanilla
1/2 tsp. Allspice
1/2 tsp. Nutmeg
3 to 4 cups Flour

Cream sugar, Crisco and margarine/butter.

Add egg, milk vanilla, cinnamon and nutmeg.

Stir in baking powder. Add flour gradually until dough is firm, not hard.

DO NOT KNEAD THE DOUGH. Roll into balls, flatten and place into pie plate. (Makes 3 tarts)

TYPICAL FILLINGS

1. Coconut
2. Guava
3. Pineapple
4. Guavaberry

UNUSUAL FILLINGS

1. Plantain
2. Prune
3. Papaya/Mango
4. Melon (the white part)
5. Tomato
6. Sorrel
7. Plumrose

Filling is made by adding sugar, cinnamon stick and vanilla. Stew over low heat until properly cooked.

Jennie Wheatley

Christmas Cassava

The cassava, a tropical plant with starchy roots, comes in three varieties; the Liah True or sweet cassava, the seven month cassava and the bitter-sweet cassava. The root of the sweet variety is boiled and used as a vegetable with fish or meat. The seven months and bitter-sweet, if cooked the same way as the sweet, are deadly poisons, but quite harmless if used in other ways. One way is the making of Cassava bread.

For this bread making you will need about 10 or 12 cassava roots, 2 large dishpans, a small bucket, a large grater, a flour bag or one yard of strong white material, a round flat iron about 2½ to 3 feet in diameter (called a baking iron), an iron hoop from a medium size barrel or cask, a flat paddle with a long handle and a fire-place large enough to hold the baking iron. In addition you will need a sifter. The best sifters are made from the sea fan or sea feather, found on most beaches.

The cassava roots are washed to remove all dirt, then scraped to remove the thick brown outer skin. After scraping they are washed again, dried and grated into one of the dish pans. This grating renders a thick white pulpy substance, called wet meal, in which there is a lot of liquid. This liquid is poisonous and has to be removed. Remove the liquid, or cassava water, by putting portions of the wet meal in the cloth and squeezing or wringing over the bucket. Repeat this process until all the wet meal is used up.

You now have a semi-dry coarse flake substance called cassava meal. This has to be sieved to remove all bits of husks or the coarse inner skin of the cassava. Place handfuls of the meal on the sea-feather sifter and shake over the open dishpan. Discard the coarse husk after sifting, and the result is a fine white meal or cassava flour.

To this flour add a small amount of fine salt, using your discretion. While you have been wringing and sifting, some member of the family should have started the fire, and by now the iron should be hot enough for baking.

As a little girl, I watched my grandmother Katie Ben test the heat of the iron by putting a small amount of meal on it, flatten it to the size of a bululboo piece and noting how soon it browned. If the iron is good and hot, you are now ready to bake the first bread. Take the hoop and place on the iron—the size of the hoop determines the size of the bread.

Put some of the meal on the iron and spread within the hoop, making it as thick as desired. After putting the meal on the iron, use the paddle to flatten or set the meal. Allow it to remain on the iron about 4 minutes or until the side is browned. If browned, remove the hoop and turn the bread over. Allow the other side to brown and remove from the iron.

This process is repeated until all the meal is used. For a variety , some shredded coconut could be placed or sprinkled on the top side of the bread before turning or it could be mixed in with some of the meal before actual baking begins.

In all sections of the country areas of Tortola, there is no Christmas without the traditional Cassava Bread and to further enhance the spirit of goodwill add the native Guavaberry liqueur and your Christmas guest will go away well satisfied.

(Note: Some of the above information was recollected by Mr. Abraham Milliner—now deceased—of St. Thomas and Jost Van Dyke and the story "Christmas Cassava" first appeared in the December 1965 issue of the VIRGIN ISLANDS VIEW)

BOILED FISH A LA CREOLE

1 qt boiling water
1 tsp lime
1 sprig chive
2-3 lbs fish
1/2 c butter
2 tbsp lime juice

1 tsp salt
1/2 onion—sliced
1 sprig thyme
1 piece hot pepper

Add salt, lime, thyme, parsley, sliced onion, chives and hot pepper to boiling water. Allow to boil rapidly before adding. Add fish and cook for 20 minutes (simmering). Fish is cooked when you begin to smell it. Remove from water. Serve with drawn butter and lime juice.

FUNGI COOKED IN COCONUT MILK

Grate coconut and extract the milk by adding enough water to make 4 cups. Bring coconut milk to boil. Add salt, cinnamon, sugar and butter. Slowly add in cornmeal, stirring constantly. Cook for 20 minutes. Remove from heat. Serve with Fish a la Creole.

Boiled sugar apple is unique to the British Virgin Islands. The sugar apple is peeled and the centre core or plug is removed. It is placed in boiling salted water. It is boiled until a knife can pass through easily and immediately removed from the water. The texture is similar to yams and some folks refer to it as steady seedy yam. Sugar apple goes well with boiled fish, cured pork and pigtail.

OUR PEOPLE SPEAK THROUGH THEIR CREATIVE EFFORTS

"The symphony of Caribbean writing has begun and the time has come for British Virgin Islanders to find their pitch and swell the harmony, thereby not only extending the literary tradition but enriching it"

(V. Penn, 1976)

OUR

PEOPLE

SPEAK

THROUGH THEIR

CREATIVE

EFFORTS

THE BRITISH VIRGIN ISLANDS NEGRO

1. No longer rise the wails of woe
No longer bleeds the dark Eboe
The planter's shell has ceased to sound
The massa's in the cold cold ground.
2. From Soper's Hole to Duckey's Bay
The Black is lord of land and sea
And title-deeds assert his right
From Norman's Isle to Soldier's Bight
3. No longer crack the drivers' whips
His sons go down to sea in ships
He never feels the oppressor's hand
His sons are owners of the land
4. No more he bows to lords he meets
His chariot rages in the streets
No more his plaintive beggar's plea
He orders on both land and sea.
5. He has forgotten his palmy plains
He has forgiven the bloody stains
No longer hears the abusive word
For Hodge's slave is Bell Vue's lord.
6. He now performs his sacred rites
Without restraint of envious Whites
His empire's battles he has fought
Gainst Prussian horde and hottentot.
7. Tell of his rise from slavery's chains
Tell of his lordship of the plains
Tell of his mastery of the sea'
Tell of his faith and charity.

A. Osorio Norman - 1885 - 1942

OUR HERITAGE

Ruins and artifacts?
Remedies and recipes?
Hair raising stories
And tall tales?
Yes these and more -
Ancient toil worn hands
Have handed down
To us and those unborn
A legacy everlasting.
An independent spirit
Born and nurtured
From the soil
Where masters saw
No worth in this dry dust
That did not yield
Abundant cotton or king sugar.
A stiff unbending Pride
Uncurbed by slavery's whip
Depression, hurricane
Shipwrecks that took our men
Struggling to keep
The seed alive.

RJennie N. Wheatley

THE FALL

I am a princess of Africa
Proud, free sister of the earth.
I express pain, laughter, famine and harvest,
Wish the dance. My first love.
Through my veins course the hot blood of passion.

My anger is like the kiss of the mamba. Powerful and deadly
And my patience is born of experience.
I rejoice in my youth, and fear only the healers' magic
And the spirits of the dead.
I am filled with the pride of my ancestors.

I am brought low.
My pride was caught but a clever façade
I have been seduced by strangers
And have become a wanderer in my own land.
My children have been scattered as many seeds in the wind.
I have sold my sons and daughters into slavery.

As I slept in the night, my face wet with tears of shame,
They took my prisoner.
Subdued, held captive like an animal
I left native Africa. In chains.

In an alien land I am led and bred like cattle. I see the mindless deaths of many of my children; Their blood being shed because of my stupidity.

I dwell in a land of a cold race.
I am forbidden the pleasure of the dance.
My pride is mere illusions.
My youth fades in sorrow, I am a beast of burden.
Forsaken and discouraged, my elders forget their magic,
They have succumbed to a new religion.

Flanked by the spirits of my ancestors
I rebel.
Feeling the stirrings of near forgotten passions
I defeat my oppressors.
I have triumphed! A Caribbean queen!

Yet, I cannot rejoice
From me has departed the memory of the dance.

I have adapted the customs of my former masters.

My old age has not begotten wisdom
Mine former captors have returned
Cunning as the mongoose, they steal my reason.
With open eyes yet blind
I have caused my land to be polluted.

The trade winds whisper warnings of the poisoning of the sea.
My children have no heritage
I downpress my brothers for my own gain
Today I strive for plenty
Knowing that tomorrow my children shall perish

I have been a princess, a slave, a queen
Now I am mere shadow of a once, mighty race.

Sheila Hyndman-Wheatley (deceased)

BAD MIND – A HUMAN DILEMMA

Nothing can wear away
A human being's God like spirit
Or corroded his fleshy heart
Like BAD MIND.
It goes by many other names
hatred, envy, malice, spite
still it's BAD MIND.
It even wears a prettier face
pretence, hypocrisy, the like
but it's BAD MIND.
And when it happens
among kith and kin
in whose blood flows
the very same genes
'tis sad.
And when that blood is drawn
by words or acts or thoughts
sometimes the killer knife
is pure BAD MIND.

Among neighbours and friends and colleagues
the dagger may be golden.

This is more dangerous
for the unsuspecting one who
seeing love where there is hate
reaches out and grasps
the golden dagger by the blade.

The wound may leave a scar
And when 'tis rubbed again
becomes a gaping sore.
This is beyond a doubt
the powerful scourge called BAD MIND.

Your house is too big
Mine too small
Your children are getting on
mine are not
why does success touch you
and leave me by the way
unkept, unhonoured, and unsung?
What have you done
that I have never done?
Those are the questionings
uttered by BAD MIND.

Is there a cure
for this destructive cancerous thought
malignant or benign?
Yes there is
a touch, a real touch of
the Master's hand
an eye that sees the neighbour
as, not better, than yourself
a Mordecai and not a Haman's heart
Can cure BAD MIND.

Jennie N. Wheatley

MANUAL TO FLICK AND CLICK

Old hard work times have changed to flick and click
With many things near to our finger tips:
The house wife had her oil and a trimmed wick
Now it is the light switch - only a flip.

Scorching coal-pots with live coals of fire
For the morning tea and round, fresh pot bread,
Same fire - routine for lunch and supper:
Just a twirl and the stove is glowing red.

Press-iron braved the live coals that did glow
Send the coal - goose stack with fire roaring;

Only to plug in — not a single blow!
Switch — it — on and the current is soaring.

From the well, water was catered in loads,
A turn water comes from the tap flowing;
Washing was scrubbing and puffing at wash – boards
Flip and a clank hear the washer rolling.

Flick and turn just the fingers exercise
Manual task kept the body fit and working;
Our ancestors were thus healthy and wise;
To make up we do skipping and jogging.

Quincy Lettsome

THE LEGACY OF OUR SEAMEN

Built from V.I. wood, manned by B.V.I. skill,
Our mariners cruised the Caribbean Sea at will;
From the coast of Cuba to the shores of Grenada
Including St. Kitts, St. Baths and Antigua.

By night a single star or constellations,
Guide them over miles to their destinations;
Circled by rain, dark clouds or a dreadful squall
The compass piloted them to their land-fall.
A glassy sea did not lock them in the bays
Though they may be weather-beaten many days;
A brisk sea – breeze and forward the boat would rave'
Rearing, jumping over each dancing wave.

During leaky, squally and cruel weather
Our sailors dared, but reefed down to a feather;
The wind whispers and they read the moving tides
Knowing those that quicken or slow the boat's strides.

Thus was carved the B.V.I. proud maritime boast
Our seafarers; greatest sailors of the coast;
Their fame etched out a marine legacy!
The world's most ingenious boaters of the sea!

Quincy Lettsome

IF BUTTA DOOHN UNDERSTAND

Ah tell Miss Butta long time
Doohn sell much of de lan',
Ah beg, ah plead, ah quarrel
But she doohn understin'.

Ah mind she 'bout she chil' run,
Fo' lawd, she got a lot;
And 'twill be so heart rending
If dey doohn get a plot.

Ah hint she how, tey fix dem
Twisters when dem cum;
Ah warn she 'bout going' stup' dy
Wild dem macooing sum.

Ah 'spleen she if der's reason
Tey let one tree or two,
Den go far inna Mount Sage
No matta who its who.

Ah show she tey ' range bus' ' ness
Tey mek lan' secure
By goin' in straight longside dem
Cash 'n lan' stan' share fey sure.

Ah tell she if tey doohn 'gree
Tey stan' longside 'o we,
Dem show dem dat she got a right
Tey protect dis paradise from plight.

Ah tell she, stick tey she wud,
Stan' firm, she mussen drain;
Doohn fall back pun de san', saw,
For she 'een drunk sell one grain.

Yuh see, we dun a custom
Tey roll pun top God san';
And lawd! We'll go tey prison
If Butta doohn understan'!

Verna Penn Moll

Gratitude

For these fair isles
In gratefulness we'll raise
Our hearts and voice
In echoing notes of prise

For these fair isles
In hopefulness we'll toil
Uniting head and hand
Enriching native soil

For these fair isles
Where duty calls we'll be;
Humble yet bold
We'll serve on, faithfully

In these fair isles
May God's glory appear
To chase away
All shady evil fear

Cho: So may we joyously unite
To swell the brotherhood
Of selfless love
That scatters all false-hood

Verna Penn Moll

Premonition

You are strong, Tortola
Not by number
Nor by power
But by the peace
Your nights can offer
You have it all, Tortola
Rise up! show forth thy splendour

Land of love, Tortola
I beg you, clear the caya
To your green valleys interior
Tortola! picturesque Tortola
Beautify your flora
Consume the cankerous sucker

Tortola, friendly Tortola
Befriend your dying fauna
Make haste! the worms gnaw at their bellies
Land by birth, Tortola
Indulge me one wee favour
Stir up your contemporary agencies

You are strong, Tortola
Not by number
Not by power
But by the peace
Your nights can offer;
You have it all, Tortola
Rise up! show forth thy splendour

Verna Penn Moll

ECLIPSE WEDDING

This is the true story of an incident that took place in the Territory on July 29 1897. The author is Mrs. Jennie Smith Wheatley, the supervisor of English at the BVI High School. Mrs. Wheatley is one of the British Virgin Islanders who are making a strenuous effort to record the history and customs of our people before they are completely lost to future generations.

Grandad Joe-Joe, you know you are always asking me to bring my tape recorder and that you will tell me a story that you want all the younger generations to remember. It's too rainy to go out today, so let me hear that story.

Uh-huh, Boysie, I remember but I have to feel in the mood to tell such a story. "Grandad, please feel in the mood today." "All right Boysie, I need my pipe and I have to sit in that old rocking chair that my mother used to sit in when she told us her story.

This is your pipe Grand Joe-Joe. Are you comfortable? Then go to town on that story.

I can see her now—my mother Leah, always with her head tied and some straw work in her hand, plaiting away as she talked. She was a gay person—her voice not soft but melodious you know—not harsh like her sister Mabel's at all. She told me the story of her wedding day so often that I know it word for word just as she told it. And when she was telling that, you dared not interrupt her or it would be trouble. I am sure if she knew you, her great grandson she would love you. In many ways you behave just like her and you even resemble her. Let's pretend Boysie, you are Joe-Joe and I am my mother Leah. Now the story.

Click! Tape recorder on Grandfather Joe-Joe.

Joe-Joe she would say I had a wedding day—Lord what a day! I was living right here in Long Look but your father came from Fahie Hill to court me. Well the wedding was July 29, 1897. I can remember it as if it were yesterday. My boy what a day! From the time morning dawn, the day was looking stormy-cloudy, windy and rainy. The sun didn't want to shine. All morning I heard Cousin Essie over in her yard bursting qua-qua. Now we didn't get on well at all. She was too mette.[1] With all her flying away and rejoicing, saying she is ready for the rapture and making plenty noise in church, she is over there saying how the Lord frowning on some people deeds and he refusing to look on their wedding. I wouldn't even answer her.

But you don't remember Cousin Essie Joe-Joe? No, you couldn't! Cousin Essie was a fine looking strapping high coloured[2] woman. They say she didn't even get married because she didn't know which one of her many admirers to choose from. I believe though that nobody was good enough for Cousin Essie. You should see her going to church on a Sunday morning. Her dress stiff with starch and sweeping the ground, her hat on two grains of hair[3].

Cousin Clara, Essie's sister was so different. She was peace to the dead[4] A short old soul with a kind face. The only time she shouted was when she had the spirit in church praising God to her heart's content. She was much darker than Essie too—a nice chocolate brown—I preferred her colour and smooth skin. Oh, Cousin Clara skin was fine and smooth!

Like I was the bride, I couldn't help but do anything, but there was so much going on. Last minute fixing up of the dress! You know everything was sewn by hand then no sewing machines at all on the island, or at least we didn't have any around Long Look. Some big people in town like the Commissioner's wife might have had one—I really don't know. But coming back to the wedding—as I was telling you, preparations were going on all around. Cakes bake and were days ago, tarts ready—the calf and the goats killed from days before. Now by 8 o'clock bad weather or no bad weather, kerosene pans of meat were cooking on the fireplaces—three rocks with woodfire between. You know man, the scent of that food was something! Hubert, your father, had send sweet potatoes from his ground in Fahie Hill, and in those days too, the wedding gifts were really different kinds of food to be prepared for the wedding. So there was food can't done[5].

Where I was now, the old head strays sometimes. Oh the morning. Yes. Well round nine o'clock my brother Benny, the one who was the sailor all down South America—that's how he got the name Bony Iris[6], you know—the sailing. Well he come and say, Leah the elements looking chook up[7], this wedding goin' have to put off. I ask Benny if he see all that food on the fire and cakes and what not in the house. But then I say to myself Benny right—he right you know. All the guests going be out there in that big trash house[8]. It build good—they won't get wet. But the trouble is the church part at East End and after the service the whole procession got to walk to Long Look. That's a good half-hour in these old long trucks, and shoes we not custom to. Anyhow, I saying to myself, I won't give Cousin Essie the satisfaction of laughing at me. My wedding going through!

Soon as I say that, 'tis like the Lord hear me and didn't like how boastful I was. The weather suddenly got worse. Round half past nine everybody in Mamy yard looking at Benny. He say he think the sun in an eclipse. You know he see things like that in the big countries when he was sailing. Even Cousin Essie with all her righteousness leaning over her fence to find out why the sun looking so. You know like how some people face look when they put on their hypocritical smile? Just like so. After Benny say that the cooks still continue with their work. For an eclipse does pass off.

My dear—round eleven o'clock some heavy clouds start to build in the East. Now this is July you remember and hurricane season so we wondering if we could keep the wedding before the storm break. This time Hubert still in Fahie Hill for he is not to see the bride before she get to the church, or else 'tis bad luck. Some of his people had come to help with the baking and cooking days before and we wondering what to do. Eh-eh, a peal of thunder come, my chile, and up to this day I feel it was an earthquake come with that clap of thunder. Some people say not, but even the old trash house was shaking.

Now this was looking serious. People start to say Benny could say what he want, but it look like Judgment Day. As soon as Cousin Clara mention Judgment Day—all those kerosene pans of food had to watch out—you should see people hauling for Bibles. I even tell Cousin Essie howdy, for I didn't want to be found on the wrong side of the Lord on that great day. Cousin Clara was frightened. But she struck up a hymn—what it was again? One of those Richard Weaver songs. It goes like this:

Judgment day is rolling round
To tell young sinners don't sin no more
Judgment day is rolling round
To tell old sinners don't sin no more

All who were not saved before got saved then. As they were on their knees,were they up again praising God. That Cousin Clara was in her seventh heaven. All these souls she was counting as stars in her crown. That would—er been some crown. She would—er go to St. Paul and those boys competition. Yes, you smile—it sounds like a joke today for we were God fearing people. Several times since that day I have asked God to forgive me for anything I do wrong on July 29, 1897.

Then a big rain come down—and brother, when that was over Benny look outside. He sing out Clara! Break up the prayer meeting! On with the wedding! The weather all right! The eclipse pass! Everybody rush out to make sure Benny wasn't fooling us. For Benny was a tricky fellow.

I was now in my glee. Time to start to fix up my bag to go to East End. I was going to get dressed at home. Look you never see fire catch up so quick under kerosene pan like now. Although Benny did cover the pans during the height of the storm some water went in, so you had to boil down that water to get the stew meat back in order. The head and foot soup was all right still. That rain water only cut down on the amount of pepper Cousin Jeaner, the head cook, put in. You see when the men got drunk at the wedding they always want peppery soup. I don't know why—so don't ask me. Ask one of the men.

Lord where I was now? Oh, I walk up East End to my godmother's house. 'Tis two o'clock now—the sun shining as it was happy to be from under the sun crossing. I didn't understand a thing and I still don't understand now, so I can't even blame it on fright. Benny also said how the amount of sin Clara got under the blood or cast into the seas of forgetfulness must be taken the burden off the sun. Even Henny, 80 years old and a half tipsy from wedding rum, claimed salvation. Eighty years is no lil bit of sin you know, and Henny wasn't exactly an angel even in her young days, Cousin Clara said. But Lord Benny would make joke even in his coffin if he get a chance. He nearly do it too.

Benny died twice in 1900. First time he died, a clap of thunder brought him back this side. We had done straighten him out and muff him. Anyhow Clara say—long time before the wedding, I telling you about—that Benny is a hell bound sinner. When the great company of believers meets, according to Cousin Clara, not many sailors going to be there. Well, I didn't hear anything particular that Benny do, but Cousin Clara should know, he and she was sex[11].

The wedding—yes—you could see your old mother's head wasn't right today. Well as I said already the sun was shining. The little flower girls were skipping up and down happy as birds for now they can dress up in their pretty clothes. Flower girl's ? No! That's wrong. Must be the bridesmaid was jumping up. Flower girls were not flourishing in 1897. The first wedding I saw flower girls to was Tommy Todman wedding 1925. 'Twas a good wedding too! But poor thing, he got drowned on the FANCY ME in 1926.

Anyhow flower girls or not somebody was skipping about happy as a lark. Everything going good till Gawdy Jess say I wonder if the parson going ride all the way from Road Town after that kind of weather. The roads must be bad. Oh Lord! I didn't think of that, but I had to hope those white ministers from England wasn't 'fraid rain like us. They wouldn't even realise it was raining, for one day in church when Parson Queely preaching he say how it is always raining in England. Man he coming! He know 'tis a wedding and how the people does prepare plenty food. Besides if it always raining in England he must be see one of these eclipse every week. He's an educated man too. He would know all about such things.

Well I was dressing and listening for horses' hoofs. Then one of the girls shout, Leah, Hubert going up now-don't look. I hear several horses going full speed up the road. Now I was wondering, Lord, he get the ring or it drop out while he riding. Several wedding I went to, somebody had to jump on a horse and go back to the bridegroom home for the ring. Pure fright you know. Men does play like they don't be nervous, but they well nervous on the wedding day, especially the kind of man who don't darken the church door till every Good Friday, Easter Sunday, and Christmas morning service.

Next shout-Leah, Parson Queely going up. Now I feel good. The wedding going to be late but it going be a wedding anyhow. Five to three and gawdy[12] Jess making last minute checks to see that I was dressed well. The walk from her house to the church only about three minutes, but it take longer for I stepping in shoes and I wasn't customs to much shoes in those days. Today I can't do without shoes. What a thing Lord! After a good bit of wriggling and ankle twisting, I reach the church. I say thank God out loud. Even Cousin Essie said she heard me. The church was packed with people. The school children were sent home during the storm, but some still lingered outside. As you know Joe-Joe, even donkey years[13] later the Methodist Church at East End was still the school for East End/Long Look children.

The ceremony was going good. I didn't cry as much as I should because I had used up my tears repenting earlier in the day. I really couldn't do much now. I want to look back to see if Cousin Essie was cutting her eyes at my back, but I have to pay attention to the parson. After all, I don't want him to think I was too stupid to understand English. And I could read and write at that. Not like some people who had to mark X because they can't write. Now I listening to the parson-will you have this man to be your Lawful wedded husband? I feel like saying, "I will" out loud not soft-soft. But this is no time for jokes, plus the Lord just show me this morning the power he got. So I answer "I will" so reverently that I sure Cousin Essie couldn't say I am a brawling young woman. And the part where the parson ask for just cause why two people can't be join in holy matrimony-that come before or after I will? No matter! I still lil worried. All the same I know we was alright or else I would er hear about it. That would er been good bone for Cousin Essie to chew on.

The ring part was the best part though. Hubert trying to pretend he isn't nervous. Well the parson had to steady his hand from trembling for Hubert to get on the ring. That's after it drop twice on the board floor, tinga-linga-ling. This time the children in the church laughing and the old ladies groaning. The loudest groan was either Cousin Clara or Cousin Essie-I couldn't tell which one. At last the ring on parson say the last prayers and we turn to come out.

Ceremony over-the whole processing leaving the church, I make sure I step out the church door first for the old people say whoever step out the church door first will going be the boss in the house. That isn't true anyhow for Hubert never one day let me push he around. So we walk Long Look. People were pitching rice for good luck especially by Gawdy Jess gate. She must be save that rice for years. All day long the road I asking Hubert how the people Fahie Hill behaved during the bad weather. He say not bad, because Uncle Jimmy had come from St. Thomas early Tuesday morning and say how the St. Thomas newspaper say[14] a eclipse coming and the weather was going to be worse around eleven o'clock. So they wasn't so frighten over there. Couple people still praying out loud, loud, but that was all. Lord if we up Long Look had know that, Cousin Clara wouldn't er have that prayer meeting. Boy people going tease her for the rest of her life, and even after.

It didn't have newspaper then you say? The Danish newspaper LA TIENDE—yes, Danish-St. Thomas, St. Croix and St. John were sold to the American Government in 1917, you know. I was there when the Danish flag come down and the United States flag went up. So much marching and speech making—'twas good though. Pass that old Bible there let me show you a copy of the paper I talking 'bout. Cousin Jimmy had bring it with him. That's July 28, 1897 ner. Read it yourself. Even had Apollo Theatre and thing like that then. Read it right there. Some weeks after the wedding my aunt Fleader who had live down there—she didn't make it to the wedding—she wasn't feeling too good—she read a newspaper for July 30, 1897. That's this one here. They lil fade out but you can make out the part telling how people behave the day before, during the eclipse. Other thing is that one too. You can make out the name Joe-Joe St. Thomas Bulletin, ner. That's it. I can't see like long time, but I can still read my Bible. Put them back in it. I save them for all the rolling years, don't lose them now. Maybe your children and children-children could see how it was in their old grandmother day.

We reach Long Look now. Mama house was pretty with flowers—the long tables had milk white table cloths. All kind of food there— dove meat of every kind, bake port, and even whelk pie. 'Twas good I telling you. The drinks, well I can't tell you the different kinds. We used to make one kind with <u>rum and lime</u>[15], but the rest were bought in St Thomas. As you would expect drinks flowing like water. Even Cousin Clara remembering the wedding at Cana of Galilee, was sipping her wine with relish. Toasts were rolling off the men tongues like oil. The best one was when Uncle Jimmy say:

Bright be the years before you
Lovers from your earliest days
May peace wave her olives o'er you
And joy attend thy ways

The music strike up now. Naturally the bride and groom had to dance the first waltz. I was no fool on my two feet and Hubert was the best dancer in Tortola. We dance and we dance and Christopher Fleming, my godfather, making that concertina talk. Hubert cousins from Fahie Hill on guitars, the triangles and the <u>Bohhaw</u>[16] were pushing music too. Then the floor open for all dancers. Well you never see just-save people dance so—waltz, polka, fox trot, seven step, two step—every one of those good old time dances. In between they serve food, but I was too happy to eat. Then Gawdy Jess come and say 'tis time to go change in your short dress to go home with your husband. Much as I wanted to dance I had to go. Mercy what a day! And we lived happily ever after—some bitter days in between, some eclipse of sun and moon in our lives too, but happily all the same... Click! The tape recorder is off!

1. inquisitive—Spanish meter "to butt in—pronounced "metay
2. mulatto
3. tilted to one side
4. no trouble at all

5. plenty
6. Buenos Aires
7. unsecured
8. thatch
9. Tie cloth under chin and around head to keep corpse's mouth closed
10. in particular
11. peers - same age
12. godmother
13. great number
14. St. Thomas Tiende Vo. 51 #66 Wednesday July 28, 1897
15. Shrub
16. Sometimes called asspipe - long piece of pipe slightly curved at bottom. Air blown in to make musical boom *without peer*

From Pass it on: A treasury of Virgin Islands tales - Jennie Wheatley

THE FOLLOWING ARE TAKEN FROM "CREATIVE ARTS IN THE B.V.I. a "FESTIVAL." All are works of Virgin Islanders and were submitted for the CREATIVE ARTS Festival sponsored by the Public Library in 1979

WHERE HIDES MY INSPIRATION

Where hides my inspiration
Doth it blend with the lush green
and homely scent
of that soursop tree?

Or with that sugar apple the fruit
pecked to expose the white flesh?
Its aroma rushing to meet my nostrils
Maybe its hidden in the joyous screams
Of the toddler
as she watches the hen
lying over her chicks?
Where hides my inspiration?

Doth it lie in days gone by
when we ran home from school
to feast on those forbidden pond apples
or the locusts which were bad for our breath
the times we filled our lunch boxes with water
to last the long walk home?

it is hidden in the painful lashes
the head teacher freely gave?

But Oh! How foolish!
my inspiration doth not hide
it seeps from the guava berries
and bitter tender apple bush
the mango juice coursing down my chin
that "devilish" Kasha bush
It is the feel of the warm tropical water

The whelks and the calabash bown
It is my joys and pains
my victories and defeats
my now and then
my inspiration is my life

Sheila Hyndman-Wheatley

COLOURFUL CALAMITY

It was Sunday, February 2, 1770, and the end of Reema's first week at Plantation Plentiful. As she sat on the flat rock below her hut, chin in hand, she was thinking that it was the first time since her arrival that she had found time to study the neighbouring huts of wattle and daub, all practically identical in shape, size –and colour. Since Monday of the past week except for an hour and a half break at noon during which she had to pick grass besides preparing her lunch, she had stood or rather stooped in line every day tying bundles of cane which were lifted onto mule drawn carts and trundled away to the factory, a short distance away. It was not strange then that everywhere her eyes rested there appeared a yellow-green blur similar to the blur one experienced after staring at a luminous object for a prolonged period.

Unfortunately for Reema, she had arrived from Africa at the height of the crop season and was immediately swept up into the "eye" of activity. At night however, the constant noise of the factory's steam engines and the creaking carts passing by laden with hogs-head of muscovado hauled by silent mules deaf to the shouts and curses of their weary drivers failed to disturb Reema's dreams of home. In fact, she slept fixed between dream and reality, the one disturbing aspect being two leering, lecherous eyes strongly resembling those of the driver in the field....

Lorna Hodge-Smith

(Excerpt from a longer story)

The Legend of The Phantom Ship

There has been many a quip
About the phantom ship.

So listen, you lubbers, and you shall hear
A quaint sea story; one without peer.

When the clouds hang low, and the night gloomy gray
A phantom ship glides into the bay

Whither she comes and whither she goes
This mystery which no one knows

She never comes when the moon is bright
But always on the darkest night

Or when the moon is on the wane
During the time of the sugar-cane

Deep in the shadow of the captain's brig
The hands they skip and dance a jig

Then the phantom crew they bend to the oar
And silently they steal ashore

Under the spreading genip tree
They hold a jumble jamboree

They skip and prance, then begin to fight
They clobber each other with all their might

In the witching hours twixt twelve and three
It is a spine-tingling sight to see

In the shadows deep, at the foot of Government Hill
Two coffins rattle, and Dry Bones battle on still

The folks who belong to Sandy Bay
Know this tale is as true as day

If you ask me how I know
Twas Uncle Charlie* told me so

(Charlie Crandall—Raconteur, author and spinner of tall tales)

Linda O'Neal

(Some of the Slogans Submitted For The Commemorative Celebration)

Freed in '34, Building our nation in '84	Lisa O'Neal
Forward be our watchword, forward in freedom forever	H. D. McBeath
Slaves of yesterday, leaders of today	Claude Kettle
We're better off now I can tell, Since Sunday Morning Well	Monique Francis
Once a chattel, but now a master Slaves in the 30's, leaders in the 80's	Lloyd Wheatley
From the abyss to the top, we have risen and will climb and never stop	Leona Harney
Slavery has been abolished Now education can flourish	Jerry Samuel
Freedom at last from the bondage of the past	Lynette Mactavious
Emancipation to progress and success	Stacy Lettsome
Our freedom today cost a lot yesterday	Dwayne Davis
The 15th decade on the freedom trail	Alexandrina A. Maduro School
Then everyone had to work, now everyone is free to work	Odean Smith
Slavery is past, our freedom is now	Vernicia Callwood
Liberated, educated and undaunted	Wayne O'Neal
Although the road was rough That just made us tough	Marissa Frett

Excerpts from

"THE LONG MARCH TO FREEDOM—GOODBYE AFRICA

(A glimpse at the Virgin Islands)by

NORWELL HARRIGAN MBE, MA, MPA, PhD, FIBA

Goodbye, Africa

They were captured, more often than not "panyared" by their own people—Mandingoe's, Koramantyns, Pawpaws, Eboes, Macoes and Angolans—dragged in chains from the hinterland of West Africa to the coast, many falling dead from heat and exertion over the long haul with only the scavenging animal life to take notice that a body along the wayside was evidence of the return to the gods of another African.

These forced marches represented the seeding and flowering of an institution—the peculiar institution—which began in the fifteenth century with two small Portuguese caravels, under orders from Prince Henry the Navigator, creeping cautiously down the Atlantic coast of Africa to a point beyond which Europeans had not heretofore ventured and returning to Tagus with the first dozen blacken taken bondage by white men. ...

The commercial exploitation of Africans, therefore, grew from a trickle to a stream, and eventually to a deluge in which first Spaniards and later French, Dutch, Danes and English contributed substantially to the flood later called the "triangular trade"—a trade which transplanted an estimated 11,000,000 blacks crazed with fear, bewildered and wretched, and which assumed colossal proportions by the end of the seventeenth century.

So did Europe come to Africa. ...

Over the years attempts have been made by officials, clergymen, and white visitors to "diagnose" the "character" of Virgin Islanders and to determine what manner of man constituted this society of black people. But their assessments have never been related to the island's historic past. What, for example, could be expected from the educational opportunities (which improved only imperceptibility) offered to men of such simplicity and ignorance. The limited land area and difficulty of literally forging a living from poor soil would surely tend towards individualism and ownership of land as a means of identity. The high incidence of litigation over it should not, therefore be surprising. Working for one's self would breed independence. Even recently dissatisfaction with conditions would elicit remarks like "I ain't forget how to plant potato;" or references to "corn grounds" and chasing a grunt tail" (fishing).

Actually, the physical evidence points to an extremely hard-working and highly intelligent people. The rugged hills which initially scared the daylights out of the first settlers, in spite of drought and hurricanes, produced food for home consumption and for sale, supplemented by the harvest of the surrounding seas. The men sailed the oceans to near and far-away places in search of work that would produce cash that would enable them consistently raise the standard of living, and housing attained the second highest level in the British West Indies without government aid of any kind. Out-migration often accompanied by terrible hardships, was not generally a means of escaping but rather a strategy for survival, through the establishment of inter-island extended household letting out appendages in order to draw on resources from a distance.

Mismanagement and neglect of the islands by the English people, both resident and at "home" (particularly the intellectual midgets sent out to administer the islands) forced the black small-holders to become, in effect, masters of their destiny in the post-emancipation period. They developed a cohesiveness in their societal relations due, at least in part, to the savagery of slavery which fostered self-help and cooperation. And economic progress, such as it was, could be ascribed largely to their ability to seize or create opportunities for advancement in the face of almost overwhelming odds. While a slave society was built on the backs of blacks, the small-holders created with their hands and by their wits a new social order—one which was stable, or at least in relative equilibrium.

After the second World War, the significant movement of people in and out of the islands, the radio contact with the American way of life in St. Thomas (often at its worst), the advent of the radio (and later television) all contributed to changes in attitudes and values, greater expectations and more sophistication; and consequently a decline in the "traditional" way of life.

With an economic boom, and at long last British Assistance there was general social advance. Housing standards, already high, moved forward by leaps and bounds; opportunities for education at all levels increased; improvements were made in public health, teachers and civil servants organized; political parties (or what passed as such) sprang up, and after 50 years the islands had an electorate and a Legislative Council, and tourism was seen as a mode of "development."

The transition from small-scale agriculture to a tourist economy, which began in the 1960's, brought an influx of immigrants, introducing, for the first time in over a century a substantial landless class whose social backgrounds differed in important respects from those of Virgin Islanders. Insofar as the normal pattern whereby immigrants occupy the lowest paying jobs did not occur, and they appeared to be getting ahead of the natives, local sentiment against the "non-belonger" began to crystallize.

The appearance of expatriate white residents associated in one way or another with the growth of investment also created difficulties, introducing the class/race patterns of association between social inequality and racial difference which portended a reversion to the social pattern of the early nineteenth century. Groups and factions which, in effect if not intent, were socially exclusive with high visibility and conspicuous affluence (in relative terms, at least) represented an affront to local sentiment leading to the cry of a "return to slavery." While to some such rhetoric appeared intemperate, irrational, irresponsible, and purely destructive in character, the fact was indisputable that there were grounds for ill-will. The islanders had to deal with a subtle form of arrogance and responsible people talked about the creation of a society whose essential features would not differ greatly from those of Rhodesia as a distinct possibility.

Thinking people in the islands then became increasingly aware of the social inequalities and the massive alienation of the local economic patrimony and many talked about "getting a piece of the action."

But few effective measures were taken to ensure that there would be any "action" to get "a piece" of. There was no doubt that although "Hodge's slave is Belle Vue's Lord," belonger was patently obvious that the bounty of nature was being destroyed, factional differences were and non-belonger and black and white had begun to set the stage for a new type of conflict. It becoming commonplace; racism was very much in evidence; economic exploitation was a fact of everyday life; and real poverty was again beginning to spread as across to economic opportunity became restricted.

Recent years have exacerbated the situation if the 1980 population figures are accepted as evidence. If immigration has not reached alarming proportions in terms of numbers, it has nonetheless put the population on the road once again to conflict. The 1980 census gives a de facto population figure of 12,034; 9,941 are black, 778 are white (up from 45 in 1960), and the remaining 443 (less 99 East Indians) appear to be of mixed or unspecified race. Of the total population 63.8 percent are "belongers." This could be interpreted to mean that the number of native Virgin Islanders is not known, since the "foreigners" given that status would be included in the belonger category. It can well be concluded that 37.2 percent of the residents of these islands are merely transients—temporary workers in a permanent economy—or those waiting for the "underground railway" to the United States.

Partly as a result of this influx of people (and there are undoubtedly other explanations as well that only empirical investigation will reveal) it can safely be said that at various levels of society today there can be found genuine contributors to the islands' economic future as well as rapacious developers determined to rob them of their birthright and leave them destitute; partners in the island's social development and cultural heritage as well as the "do-gooders" with an eye on the main chance, organizing to improve what they do not understand and to establish what is not needed and those who love the islands and are prepared to defend them against all comers, as well as native "quislings" who would sell them for a mess of pottage; and expatriates and natives, belongers and non-belongers, whites and blacks who don't give a damn one way or the other.

VIGILATE

One hundred and fifty years after the abolition of slavery the Virgin Islands are one again on the verge of dramatic changes if worldwide trends are any indication. As they approach the bicentennial and the twenty-first century, the islands' motto should become their watchword, "VIGILATE" (Watch)!

As Weldon Johnson reminds us (in what is now called the Negro National Anthem) "We have come... out of the gloomy past

Over a way that with tears have been watered

Treading our path through the blood of the slaughtered..."

And what is needed today is another 1853. This time an upheaval of ideas—a war, so to speak, to be waged in the minds and hearts of every Virgin Islander. As we fight for a still brighter tomorrow, and freedom in a more real sense, Johnson's prayer should never be forgotten:

"Shadowed beneath Thy hand
May we forever stand
True to our God
True to our native land"

Tales for Future Historians

(From September, 1942 issue of "VIRGIN ISLANDS OFFICIAL BULLETIN" by E.L. Bacon)

When J.B. Nissen set out from St. Thomas one day in 1797 for Surinam in the Danish brig MINERVA, with eight other vessels under convoy of a Danish ship-of-war, he was worried and nervous. The seas were almost as unsafe as they are today when German submarines are ravaging shipping in the Atlantic and the Caribbean. In all directions privateers were prowling about and capturing cargo ships. He was not at all sure he was going to Surinam, but he did not like to think of the dangers of the voyage. He was a man of peace, who when he was not trading between the islands worked as a church missionary.

It was toward evening when the MINERVA was captured by a small privateer from Tortola. The privateer was a schooner called the "LITTLE ARCH" with between 20 and 25 men onboard. She was owned by Dr. Bartlett of Road Town, and was commanded by Captain Barnett.

Says Nissen in his diary: "Captain Barnett was a brisk young fellow. The night they took us he made a leap from the schooner's mast on board our brig with a sword in his hand." The MINERVA was taken into Road Town, where her cargo was confiscated. Nissen who owned part of the cargo, protested, but the English gave no satisfaction. However, in other respects, they treated him well, and he was entertained in some of Road Town's best homes where he admired the handsome silverware and the luxurious furnishings. The English entertained lavishly. There were many rich families, some of them had made fortunes from sugar plantations and cotton. Raw cotton was then bringing $64 a bale. Thirty-five years later it was down to $6, but privateers were growing rich just as fast as the sugar and cotton growers.

The manuscript of Nissen's diary is now owned by Louis M. Monsanto of Krum Bay, St. Thomas and has been in his family for several generations. It should be of value to future historians in their effort to reconstruct the past of these islands. So far there is not much authentic material for history. It would probably be impossible to write more than a few pages of it without resorting to legend or dull official records which may be in Government archives in London. The historian needs more than official records to make his book interesting. He must give an intimate account of the people of the by-gone generation. He needs memoirs, diaries, old letters, all kinds of information in which Government is not interested. But everything of that sort has been swept away by hurricanes, or destroyed by fire, or taken to England by the people most concerned. It is chiefly the hurricanes which have made the future historian's job difficult. They have swept away not only most of the records but have left nothing but a few broken walls of the fine old houses. How little we know of the people who were here in the early days. Some old-timers tell stories they heard from their grandparents, who heard them from even earlier generations, but such stories, whenever put into writing, become distorted, each generation making them a little more inaccurate.

But the broken walls tell stories, too. There is that ruin on the top of Joe's Hill for example, which is all that remains of the home of Sir Arthur Rumbold. Enough of the walls remain to indicate that it was a fine pretentious house. Now the trail goes through the rooms where Sir Arthur entertained. He came here as Commissioner in 1868. A few old people still remember that he lived in what to Tortola of those days was a good deal of luxury.

He must have had private means. It is not likely that the Government built that house for him away up on that hill top.

There is a story that he built a road so that he could drive in his carriage to the village. He was comparatively a recent character in the island's history, yet after only 74 years, scarcely anything is known about though some future historian might possibly find a good deal in England, where he may have descendants. He sounds interesting. There is something about him that stirs the imagination: What were his entertainments like? Were there gay dances in the hilltop house? Were there romances in the family? Was there a beautiful daughter who eloped with the poor young mate of a merchantman? Material for a novel may have lain in what we don't know and perhaps will never know about the Rumbold family.

R.A.F. AWARD

(Printed in the April 1942 issue of the BULLETIN as extracted from the LONDON TIMES)

Brilliant work of bomber crews. The King has approved the following award in recognition of gallantry and devotion to duty in the execution of Air operations:-

DISTINGUISHED SERVICE ORDER
Flight Llety. C.L. ROY, 150 SQD.

"He has carried out his attacks with consistent skill and courage. As a captain he has contributed much to the squadron's repeated successes, maintaining morale at a very high level. His operational sorties as Captain have included six raids on Cologne and five on Hamburg."

Flight Lieutenant CHARLES ROY is the second son of The honorable William Campbell Roy and Mrs. Roy of Tortola, and spent several of his boyhood's years with his parents in Tortola. Mr. and Mrs. Roy are justly proud of their son's fine achievement and have our heartiest congratulations on the high honour which has been conferred on him. William Roy, the eldest son is a Captain in the Army somewhere out East. The youngest son, Rowan, is in Lakefield Preparatory School, Ontario, where he is a keen Naval cadet.

AL SAYSRB

For further information on Rowan Roy

See LIFE NOTES by Joseph Renold O'Neal

Mr. O'Neal was interviewed by Xandra Adamson

Bohog put in gol' teet'

By Meston Malone Student of the B.V.I. High School

PROVERBIAL SAYINGS

"WHEN PUSSY BELLY FULL HE SAY RATTA STING"

(NOT SO CAT WALK — G. Seaman)

WE

HAVE

OUR

OWN

PROVERBS

WATER "WHEN YO RUN FROM JUMBIE YOU MEET COFFIN"

PROVERBIAL EXPRESSIONS

These are the wise sayings that our older generations speak. Sometimes they are so deep that the younger generation does not understand them. Sometimes they are graphic enough to afford some insight. "Water more than flour" is clear, but "'Tis goat good heart mek dem tail behind dem back" takes us a while to figure out that too much kindness can result in poverty.

BoHog put in gol' teet 1974

Revised edition 2004

A PERSON'S PLACE IN SOCIETY

(A) WHEN PAPAW TREE FALL DOWN, NANNY GOAT JUMP OVER HE
(1) When a person falls from high circumstances to low anyone can disregard him

(A) DONKEY GOT NO BUSINESS IN HORSE RACE
(1) A person ought to keep within his own class or group in society

(A) BO(AR) HOG DOES PUT IN GOL(D) TEET(H) TO MAKE YOU T(H)INK HE'S A GENTLEMAN
(1) One puts on a certain veneer in order to appear refined or dignified.

(A) LAY DOWN WID DOG; YO(U) GE(T) UP WID FLEAS
(1) Mixing with people below one's level, tarnishes the reputation

(A) ROCKSTONE DOWN RIVER BOTTOM DON(T) KNOW WHEN DE SUN HOT
(1) The person living in opulence doesn't know anything about poverty

Time

(A) E(V)ERY HALLELUJAH GOT A AMEN
(1) The best of everything comes to an end

RELATIONSHIPS

(A) SOURSOP TREE DON(T) BEAR APPLE
(1) What a person is what we expect of him because of his parentage.

(A) WHA(T) HU(R)T EYE MEK NOSE RUN WATER
(1) What effects one member of a family adversely, hurts all the rest.

ADVICE

(A) IF YO(U) GOT COCOA IN DE S UN YO(U) GOT TO LOOK OUT FO(R) RAIN
(1) Where there is a possibility of trouble one should be extremely anxious and alert

(A) WHEN YO(U) BROTHER BED BU(R)NING, PUT YOURS IN SOAK
(1) When disaster has already struck someone, take extra precautions to avoid the same predicament

(A) WHA(T) SWEETEN GOAT MOUT(H) BITTER HE TAIL
(1) The beginning may be pleasant, but the final outcome rather unpleasant

(A) E(V)ERY SHUT EYE AIN(T) SLEEP
(1) Be careful, since things are not always as they appear on the surface

(A) HOWE(V)ER FOREDAY RUN MORNIN(G) GOIN(G) CATCH (H)E

(1) A person who commits an offence and is not detected is encouraged to continue doing wrong, but is generally caught because he becomes overconfident of his safety.

(A) YO(U) COULD HIDE DE FIRE BU(T) WHA(T) YO(U) GOIN(G) DO WI(D) DE SMOKE?

(1) You cannot conceal or destroy all traces of evidence for what is done in darkness sooner or later comes to light.

(A) WATER BOILING FO(R) FISH AN(D) FISH AIN(T) KNOW

(1) A person does not know that trouble is brewing for him:

(A) SHIP WHA(T) DON(T) RULE BY DE RUDDER DE ROCK GOIN(G) PICK IT UP

(B) WHEN YO(U) KETCH (CATCH) YO(U) COL(D) YO(U) GOIN(G) BEAR YO(U) COUGH

(C) WHA(T) PORK DON(T) SEASON DOES SMELL (1) People who refuse to take advice must be prepared to suffer

(A) TROUBLE TREE DON(T) BEAR NO BLOSSOM

(1) Trouble doesn't send out warning signals

(A) DE OLDER DE RAM, DE STIFFER DE HORN

(1) Experience comes with age

(A) DE OL(D) STEER (GE(T) SUSPICIOUS WHEN DEM FEED (H)E TOO HIGH

(1) When those in authority begin to act unusually pleasant they are planning to get rid of you

(A) GAULIN(G) SAY TRUS(T) NO CLOUD

(1) Every man is an enemy

(A) LONG GRASS CARRY NEWS

(1) Trust no one

(A) ONE MANGY GOAT SPOIL DE WHOLE FLOCK

(1) One defective sample will spoil the whole lot

(A) SHUT YO(U) DOOR AN(D) LICK YO(U) CHIL(D)

(1) Deal with your personal affairs privately

(A) SHIT DON(T) CARE WHO HE DAUB

(1) Bad company doesn't care who comes under its influence

(A) E(V)ERY STINKING CHEESE GOT (H)E OWN BREAD

(1) No matter how bad the person or thing, there is someone who will want him or it

(A) DEAD MAN CAN(T) CARRY DEAD UP DE HILL

(1) The helpless cannot give help just as the blind can't lead the blind

(A) TAKE HALF-A-BIT TO BUY TROUBLE AND IT TAKE DOUBLOON TO CLEAR IT

(1) "Had-a-know" means if "I had known." Therefore, if the person had anticipated the outcome of his actions he would have acted differently.

(A) TAIN(T) GOT NO TREE IN DE SEA

(1) There is nothing to hold on to therefore one ought to be fully equipped in case of danger

(A) WHEN MAN DEAD GRASS GROW BEFORE HE DOOR

(1) When the owner is not there to oversee things they are not done properly

(A) TWO CONGER CAN(T) LIVE IN DE SAME HOLE

(1) Two people of equally difficult temperaments hardly get along well

(A) TIS WHO IN DE HOUSE KNOW WAY (WHERE) DE LEAK IS

(1) Whoever has the problem knows the real difficulty

(A) TIS GOAT GOOD HEART MEK DEM TAIL BEHIN(D) DEM BACK

(1) Because of a person's kindness and willingness to help others, he will always be poor

(A) DOG DON(T) BITE AT DE FRON GATE

(1) Some people do things in an underhand manner

(A) CATTLE MIN(D)ER KNOW CATTLE TEMPER

(1) The person who deals with the situations constantly ought to understand it best

(A) DON(T) SAY MORE WID YO(U) MOUT(H) THAN YO(U) BACK CAN STAN(D)

(1) Don't accept more responsibility than you are able to carry

(A) WHO GOT DE WATCH GOT TO KEEP DE LOOK OUT

(1) The person in charge must always be on the look out

(A) RUN FROM JUMBIE YO(U) MEET UP COFFIN

(B) TAKE CARE YO(U) MISS DE BASIN AN(D) HIT DE POE (CHAMBER POT)

(1) Same as jumping from the frying pan into the fire, i.e. from bad to worse

(A) MAN WORK, DOG REAP

(1) A few persons work but everyone received the benefit

(A) DON(T) LOOK FO(R) BLACK SHEEP IN A DARK NIGHT

(1) Don't put off an issue until it's too late

(A) WHO PUT FOWL TO MIN(D) CORN?

(1) It is pointless putting a thief to guard possessions

(A) TAIN(T) HAVE FO(R) GRAVE DIGGER – CARPENTER WORSE

(1) This expression means having nothing at all. For while the grave is absolutely necessary for burial, the coffin is not.

(A) YO(U) PISSIN(G) ON HOT ROCK AND SMELLIN(G) IT

(1) You are being insolent

(A) WEDDING CAKE AIN(T) POTATO

(1) Suggests the difference between the rare (cake) and the common-place (potato)

(A) YO(U) BROKE A STICK TO CUT YO(U) OWN BACKSIDE

(1) You prepared your own downfall

(A) SI(T) DOWN NEVER SAY GET UP

(1) If you relax when you ought to be working you'll never feel like working again

(A) LIE DOWN AIN(T) NO REST, BUT SI(T) DOWN IS LESS

(1) An exaggerated plea for complete relaxation

(A) STUDIATION BEAT EDUCATION, BUT STARVATION BEAT (TH)EM ALL

(1) Studiation is knowledge gained by "studying yo(u) head." It's a rare brand of smartness, not acquired from formal studying.

(A) BETTER BELLY BUS' DAN GOOD FOOD GO TO WAS(T)E

(1) Eat all you can

(A) DA (I)S ONLY DE COTTA; DE BUN BEHIN(D)

(1) That's merely the light beginning – the real trouble is behind.

(A) COOL TREE CATCH RUNAWAY NIGGER

(1) Comforts will make one forget that he is in danger of being punished

(A) DOG WHA(T) BRING BONE IN YO(U) YARD GOIN(G) CAR(RY) OUT BONE

(1) If someone brings news to you that same person will carry out news.

ATTITUDES

(A) IN FRONT DOG TIS "MR DOG," BEHIN(D) DOG TIS "DOG"

(1) In a person's presence politeness is evident - in his absence one says anything

(A) WHEN SAUCEPAN OPEN EVERY MAN JACK PEEP

(1) When a secret gets out every everybody is interested in gossiping about it

(A) GROUND LIZARD KNOW WHA(T) HE DO, GOD ALMIGHTY MEK HE CAN(T) LOOK UP

(1) Sometimes a person who has a weighty conscience can't face the person whom he has wronged.

(A) FISH TRAP DON(T) MAKE NOISE, BUT IT DO GOOD WORK

(1) A person's effectiveness is not measured by the amount of noise he makes

(A) TAIN(T) DE COW DAT BAWL DE MOS(T) DOES WAN(T) DE MOS(T) WATER

(1) The person who begs most does not necessarily have the greatest need

(A) FINGER DON(T) POINT IN, DEM DOES POINT OUT
(1) A person does not accuse himself

(A) HOG KNOW WAY TO ROOT
(1) Any person knows to meddle or stir up trouble where there will be least resistance

(A) MONKEY NEVER CLIMB SAND BOX TREE
(1) Sensible people keep out of danger

(A) IF WIN(D) DON(T) BLOW YO(U) WON(T) SEE FOWL UNDER CLO(TH)ES
(1) You won't know the real circumstances until something happens to upset the normal course of events
(2) When things are bad you are quiet, but when things improve you make plenty noise

(A) GIVE H(IM) BASKET TO CARRY WATER AND SEA FEATHER TO DIP IT UP
(1) Ask a person to do the impossible

(A) I DON(T) WAN(T) TURKEY WHEN HE WING BROKE
(1) I don't want anything defective no matter how valuable it is

(A) YOU CAN MAKE TWO MOUNTAINS MEET WAY (WHERE) TWO TOE NEVER TOUCH
(1) You were capable of carrying tales between two persons who were never likely to quarrel without your aid

(A) YOU ARE LIVING CHEAP AND SMELLING SWEET
(1) You are a parasite

(A) YO(U) HAVE MO(RE) FRONT "N KATIE BEN
(1) Front here means initiative and also being forthright

(A) ONE FOWL LAY DE EGG; NUDDER (ANOTHER) FOWL GOIN(G) RAISE DE CHICKEN
(1) Said in the case of questionable paternity

Miscellaneous

(A) E(V)ERY DOG GOT HE DAY AND E(V)ERY BITCH HER SUNDAY
(1) Each person experience good or bad fortune at some time

(A) YO(U) CLEANING GROUND FO(R) MONKEY TO RUN ON
(1) You are making circumstances easier for others

(A) YO(U) WENT TO SCHOOL TO SLEEP ON DE BENCH
(1) You are completely illiterate

(A) WHEN MARY DOING WELL, MARTHA KETCHING HELL
(1) While some are enjoying life others are experiencing difficulties

(A) WHER(E) A HORSE TIE HE GOT TO FEED
(1) A person must be sustained with his work or place of abode

(A) IT HAVE SOMETHING IN DE MORTAR BESIDES DE PESTLE

(1) Something is going on which one does not want to admit

(A) BORROW PETTI COAT AIN(T) GOT NO STRING

(1) Implies that borrowing is a poor method of obtaining anything, Coat here means a petti-coat that was kept up at waist by means of string, and not elastic

(A) BILL STRONG FO(R) WATERISH PUM(P)KIN

(1) Expresses the same idea as "Hog know way to root," Since a waterish pumpkin will offer no resistance to the bird's beak

(A) WATER CAN(T) STAN(D) UP ON CLIFF

(1) Water is no use to a hungry man: it doesn't sustain

(A) WHA(T) GO OVER HORSE BACK COME UNDER HE BELLY

(1) One cannot escape the consequences of one's action

(A) TAIN(T) DE WORD DOES HURT, BU(T) DE ANSWER

(1) The meaning is obvious

(A) HAN(D)SOME GIRL GO(T) DIRTY TRICKS

(1) Appearance are deceptive

(A) WHA(T) YO(U) EXPEC(T) FROM A BAG OF COAL BU(T) DUS(T)

(1) The poor behaviour exhibited is not surprising

(A) BAD BREAD GOOD IN SCARCE TI ME

(1) When there is dire necessity even that which was despised becomes valuable

(A) DEM TWO IS CHAMBER-POT AND BACKSIDE

(1) They are very close friends

(A) BOIL YAM WILL GROW NOW

(1) Very common expression used when there is a lot of rain and certainly suggests that anything planted will grow

(A) WHA(T) DE GOOD O(F) SHIP ON DRY LAN(D)

(1) What point is there having the most valuable thing if it is in a place where it cannot be used.

"HAPPINESS GROWS AT OUR OWN FIRESIDES

AND NOT TO BE PICKED IN STRANGERS GARDENS"

Douglas Jerrold

(from BEST QUOTATIONS FOR ALL OCCASIONS)

AT HAPPY TIMES WE CELEBRATE

AT

HAPPY

TIMES

WE

CELEBRATE

Weddings of Long Ago

"Weddings of Long Ago" was written by Aston Archibald in 1973. The primary source of his information was Mrs. Rubena Connor, (1912-1974), a great old-timer and former teacher. Mrs. Connor, who had lived through earlier times, would have seen some of her peers being married and we imagine with what pleasure and nostalgic élan she recounted those weddings. I am sure most of the details could have come from her own experiences. Did the ceremony mean more then than it does now?

Weddings of long ago, dating as far back as fifty years were in many ways different from weddings of today's.

In those days weddings were usually held on Wednesdays and that day was termed "wedding day". The wedding ceremony took place in the morning between ten and ten -thirty.

After the ceremony, the wedding party walked to the home of the bride regardless of how near or far it was, as there were no vehicles available for transportation then. Sometimes they even got wet on the way. Late guests sometimes rode on horses, mules or donkeys depending on how far the journey was. Onlookers threw many pounds of rice at the party as it passed by.

On arrival at the bride's home, relatives and friends would congratulate the bride and groom, shake their hands and sometimes kiss them. Guns were also fired in honour of the marriage. The celebrations usually began again around 2:30 p.m. The bands consisted of an accordion or music box, a drum, a guitar, a squash, a pipe and a steel frame known as "the triangle". The guests and other workers who had helped with the preparation, would dance far into the night, or until they were tired.

Weddings in those days lasted from Wednesday to Saturday midnight. Some of the guests stayed for everything and often made themselves comfortable sleeping on floors or any convenient place.

On the morning after the wedding, it was the duty of the bride's mother to take breakfast to the married couple and ask her son-in-law pertinent questions. This was also the day when trays of cakes (sliced and put in saucers) would be sent far and near to relatives and friends and even to some folks who had attended the wedding.

In my opinion "Weddings of Long Ago" was very exciting.

by Aston Archibald

Straight from US Vol. 1 No. 2

Harvest Festival

Told by Irene Pickering

(To her sons Kedrick and Arlington Pickering)":

When harvest time was approaching there was much excitement. During the week preceding Harvest Sunday this excitement reached fever pitch. There would be practic of recitations and songs and learning how to march properly.

Then on Friday evening everyone met at the church and the programme was presented just as it would be done on Sunday. At the end of the programme we went outside into the yard, picked flowers and marched up the aisle as the choir sang "Lord of the Harvest." We were taught when to raise our gifts and when to turn around to present them.

On Saturday evening we went to the church again with flowers and palm branches to decorate the church. Gifts of sugar cane and coconuts were also placed in the corners of the church and on the windows.

On Sunday morning there was the usual eleven o'clock service. A number of visitors arrived in time for this service. There were no cars then and people came from far and near walking, riding on horses, mules, sailing in rowing-boats or sloops and later by motor launch. Because of the means of transportation, many people brought their good clothes and dressed in their friends' homes. Interest in the actual harvest programme was so high that after service many people stayed behind until harvest time never leaving their seats until the programme was over.

The programme was very similar to what it is today – songs and recitations being in the usual fare. The highlight of the programme was the harvest march which is unique to the Methodist churches of the British Virgin Islands. No one can ever forget the song of the harvest march.

CHORUS

Lord of the harvest, Father of mercy,
Triune Jehovah, Thine be the praise,
Crowning the year with Thy goodness and mercy
Songs of thanksgiving to Thee we'll raise.

(1)

Corn we are bringing, gilded with sunshine
Gift to our God to the hungry and poor;
Type of our Saviour, the true bread from heaven,
Feed us with that bread, O Lord, evermore.
(At this point the marchers offer up corn, bread, cakes, tarts and candies)

(2)

Great blushing fruits from the orchards' abundance
Sweetly fulfilling the promise of spring,
This is our offering—Father receive it,

May we be fruitful in every good thing.
(As the words indicate, the offering of vegetables and fruits is made here)

(3)

Fair Rose of Sharon, flowers we bring Thee
Clad in the beauty of colour and light,
Though they have toiled not, thy hands yet have blessed them,
And in their beauty thou takest delight.

(The final offering is of bouquet of flowers)

After a full day of visiting, the sounds of horses' hoofs could be heard departing from the village. Many of us were given short rides on horses and frequently we accompanied friends who were walking as far as Little Dix Hill.

On Monday morning there was no school for there had to be a harvest sale. (There were no school rooms at East End in those days as all schools were kept in churches). After everything was sold, the church was swept, and the yard cleaned in readiness for school next day.

MRS. LEONA LETTSOME CRABBE PLAYED ACCORDION AND HARMONICA

Old Time Concerts and Tea Meetings

Most of the present generation has not heard of the Concerts and Tea meetings which formed part of the culture of their parents and grandparents. And if they have heard, they certainly have not experienced them. The old time Concert and Tea-meeting were among the high points of entertainment up until about 40 years ago. The only difference between the two being the "tea" which was served at the Tea-Meeting.

The programme for these important occasions included "dialogues" – now we call them "plays" – written by the local playwrights, recitations by children or adults and songs. The songs included choruses, solos, duets, and quartets. Many of the recitations were locally composed poems, the funnier the better.

A "Practice Master" was sought who would be in charge of rehearsals. He was usually someone in the community who had recognized leadership and creative ability. Often he was the same person who wrote the plays and poems.

After the programme everyone danced to the music of the local band-fungi band until the wee hours of the morning. At the Tea meeting, however, tea was served before the dancing began. The "tea" was, of course, "cocoa tea", with tart, and sometimes pound cakes as well. Some of the recitations and songs used at these Tea meetings are below.

Voice of Golda Malone

ANNIE GIVE BACK THE RING

The dress done mek and the house done furnish
Annie give back the ring
The dress done mek and house done furnish
Annie give back the ring

The bann done publish the guest invited
Annie give back the ring
The bann done publish the guest invited
Annie give back the ring
The egg done bus and the poun cake rising
Annie give back the ring
The egg done bus and the poun cake rising
Annie give back the ring

What the devil ah going tell Mr. Bently
Annie give back the ring
What the devil ah going tell Mr. Bently
Annie give back the ring

NOW I WISH I WAS SINGLE AGAIN

When I was single I lived at my ease
Now I married a husband to please
Four small children to maintain
Oh how I wish I was single again

First thing at night is mama I want to go to bed
First thing in the morning is mama I want a piece of bread
Next thing is mama I have a pain in my head
Oh how I wish is was single again
For a man is like a blue bird
That flies from tree to tree
And when he meets with other girls
He thinks no more of me.
From Golda Malone's Collection

I LONG TO BE SINGLE AGAIN

My wife has the fever
And I hope it won't leave her
For I long to be single again

I sent for the doctor O then
The doctor did come O then
And I long to be single again

My wife she died O then
I laughed until I cried
To know that I was single again

The music did play at the funeral O then
And I danced all the way
To know that I was single again

I married another O then
I married another she was worse than the other
I long to be single again

Golda Malone

AS I WAS AWALKING

As I was awalking one bright summer day
To the parliment garden to hear the band play

The finest damsel I ever did see
She walked along quickly and came up to me

Young man, Youngman don't think I am bold
For I am the darling of the night I have been told
Come along quickly and let's take a walk.
To enjoy the fine breeze on a pleasant sea walk
We shook hands in hand and we both went away
It was not very long when we both did agree
We went along hugging and pressing so dear

Young man, young man see what you've done
Because I've encourage a few moment play
Mother will be angry and she will be right
She'll treat me quite harshly and cause me to cry.

Young man, young man marry must we
Don't leave me to grieve for love I pray thee
How can I marry you when I have a wife
She is the dear darling damsel and the pride of my life.

Golda Malone

ONE SUMMER MORNING

One Bright Summer morning as I was awalking
One bright summer morning as I was awalking
Whom think should I meet up my fair darling damsel
She wrapped up in flannel as cold as could be

Oh come dearest mother sit down beside me
Oh come dearest mother and pity my cry
For my poor heart is breaking my poor head is bending
I'm seeking salvation and surely must die

Do send for the young man that first introduce me
Do send for the young man that put me in pain
Do send for the doctor although it is too late
For I am a young girl cut down in my pride

Six jolly young sailors to carry my coffin
Six jolly young sailors to walk by my side
With a bunch of red roses to place on my coffin
That the people might smell me while walking along.

Golda Malone

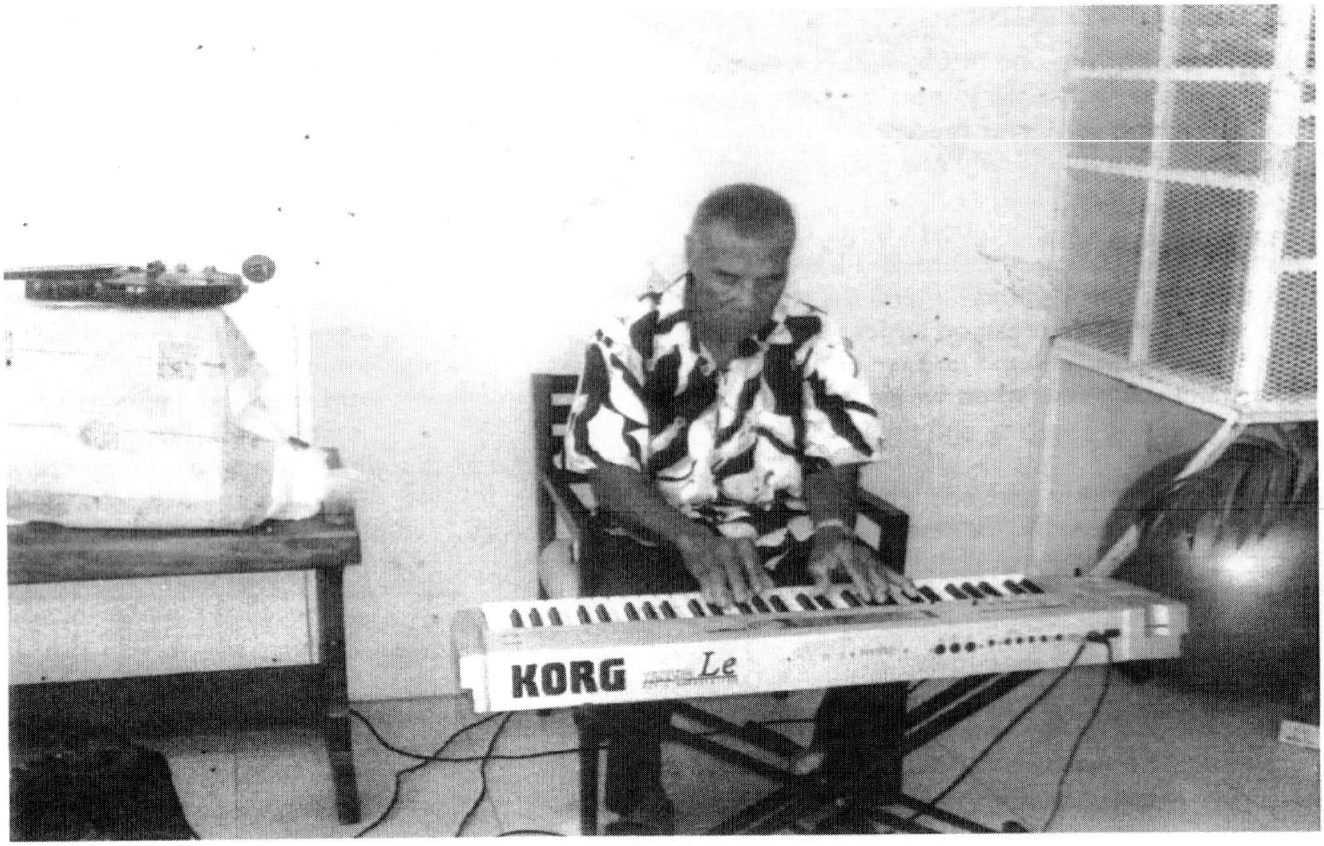

MR. BERRISFORD SMITH PLAYING KEYBOARD HE PLAYED ACCORDION AND HARMONICA AS WELL

ONE NIGHT WHEN THE WIND DID BLOW COLD

One night when the wind did blow cold
Blow bitter across the wild moor
Poor Mary she came with her babe in her arm
Wondering back to her dear father's home

Dear father dear father she cried
Have pity on me I implore
For the babe in my arm it will perish and die
From the wind that blow across the wild moor

The old man was deaf to her cry
Not a sound did not reach to his ears
But the watch dog did bark and the village bell toll
From the wind that blow across the wild moor

Oh how did the poor old man feel
When he open the door in the morn
And he saw Mary dead but the babe still alive
From the wind that blew across the wild moor.

Golda Malone

MR. TIMOTHY

One morning one morning one morning in May
I spied a fair damsel she looked in dismay
She is my true love she's gone far away
I have taken leave of her since yesterday.

The first time I met her she was at a ball
She vowed and consented to marry me
She asked me my name and I made my reply
MR. T-I-M-O-T-H-Y.

Now tell me my darling if you love me true?
Will you be my wife both tender and true?
So let us prepare and go to the Church
And don't mind your old F-A-T-H-E-R.

They went to the church and got married they say
She went to her father the very next day Dear father,
Dear father, I've come to let you know
That I'm M-A-R-R-I-E-D.

The old man he grumbled and looked at me so
You've married my daughter the only dear one
But since it is so I must really comply.

August Monday 1964

From somewhere in the nearby yard a rooster crows his salute to the dawn as the sun in all its brilliance slowly rises over Peter's island. The air is cool and it's very still with a feeling of tension in the atmosphere as if the island is holding its breath.

This stillness is suddenly broken by the strains of the "ST. KITTS ROAD MARCH" as a band comes down the street signally the start of the "RISE AND SHINE" tramp. The music calls sleepers from their beds, for its AUGUST MONDAY in Tortola, the start of the annual festival.

A group of hardy souls, mostly young men on their way home from the midnight dance have joined the early risers and it's obvious they are ready for the big day ahead. The sun moves higher in the sky and the members of troupes and floats have begun to arrive with costumes representing all the colors of the rainbow.

A cry of "here comes the Queen" is heard and the Queen's float can be seen approaching. You can only gaze in amazement at the beauty of it. It is completely covered with flamboyant and every colour this profusion of reds, yellows, whites and pinks are small branches of the royal palm, whose green fronds set all the other colours off to perfection.

The Queen herself is a confection in white and gold. Her dress is embroidered with gold seed beads and has about 9 yards of lace forming a train which also sparkles with gold beads. She carries a large white ostrich plume which she waves at the applauding crowd.

Everywhere is the music of the calypso as each troupe has its own band of musicians. The air is filled with the sound of shouted directions, the creak of saddles as the cavalcade riders get their horses in line and the sound of music is heard above all other sounds.

By then the parade is ready to leave with the gaily decorated cavalcade in the lead. This is followed by the Queen and her Court, the Majorettes, troupes and costumed individuals, all interspersed with Steel Bands and other orchestras.

One troupe portrays a scene from the movie "QUO VADIS". To look at this group you wonder if they are trying to dazzle or outshine the tropical sun; there is such a splash of diamonds, rhinestones, and assorted "jewels" on the costumes. The soldiers, forming the guard, seem to have been handpicked from the Praetorium guard of Imperial Rome. The Senators, Ladies and Citizens all appear languid and world weary as if they truly lived in that decadent age.

As the many groups pass by your eye is caught by a troupe of ten young men from Baughers Bay who bear the sign "EVEN THIS IS STYLE". Their costumes are the last word in originality. They are made from leaves of the local "pain-killer" tree. These leaves are stitched together to form a shift-like garment. A hat, also made from leaves is part of each costume, and the 'piece de resistance is an extremely large leaf umbrella that actually opens and closes. The crowd wildly applauds as the boys open and close this giant leaf parasol.

The stirring beat of the calypso is everywhere as the various groups dance their way to the Recreation Ground where the demonstrations and pole plaiting contest will take place. There are four groups in the "plait pole" competition and by far the most outstanding in costume is the group bearing the name of the "DOMINOES." The whole group is dressed in black and white with large dominoes painted on the backs of shirts and blouses. The pole is painted black and white and the dancers hold black and white ribbons. As they begin to weave the intricate pattern of the spider web, all twelve couples dancing in unison, the large crowd is fascinated beyond words. The only sound is the music of Sparrows. "ROYAL JAIL."

The pole competition is coming to a close and the crowd is getting ready to go dancing down to the market where they will purchase sticks, candles and Japanese lanterns for the torch-light procession which begins at eight o'clock. When the procession is finally finished, those who are able will attend one of the many dances at the clubs or go home to rest tired feet. Whatever they do, the revelers will remember this day for its beautiful weather, the glorious riot of color that comprised the parade, and the melody and beat of the calypso –that music that complements and completes every West Indian festival.

Submitted for a Creative Writing Class by Eileene L. Parsons 1967

ENSOR WALTER SMITH
18 November, 1907 – 12 June, 1984

MRS. JOSEPHINE ROMNEY SMITH

FIRST MS BVI – IRENE PENN, 1975

EVERYBODY LOOKING FOR THEIR ROOTS!!
"QUEEN IRENE" OWN RIGHT HERE
SHIS IS FLANKED BY HER GRANDPARENTS

FOLK SONGS

CAPTAIN WHAT'S YOUR CARGO

Captain what's your cargo,
I lay, I low
Only dry bread and tobacco
I lay, I low.

I bring my book and bible,
I lay, I low
You could read it you able
I lay, I low.

NANCY BANANA IS MY BANANA

Nancy banana is my banana
Cedo boy, Cedo
Nancy banana is my banana
Cedo boy, Cedo.

Nancy banana is your banana
Cedo boy, Cedo
Nancy banana is your banana
Cedo boy, Cedo.

Nancy banana is two for a penny
Cedo boy, Cedo
Nancy banana is two for a penny
Cedo boy, Cedo.

MISS KITTY

I meet Miss Kitty in the morning sun
Heave away boy, heave away
I ask her what's the matter with her eye
Heave away boy, heave away.

She say the dew fall down and blind she eye
Heave away boy, heave away
She say the dew fall down and blind she eye
Heave away boy, heave away.

ELLA GIFT

Sonny Henley wey yo find deh rum
Into Ella Gift pantelet
Sonny Henley wey yo find deh rum
Into Ella Gift pantelet

Oveh deh side, ovah deh side
She toss her pantalets ovah board
Oveh deh side, ovah deh side
She toss her pantalets ovah board

Ella Gift was a wutless woman
To hide the rum in her pantalets
But when she geh by the "COW and the CALF"
She toss the pantalets oveh board

Sonny Henly was a wutless man
To find the rum in her pantalets
Sonny Henly wey you find deh rum
Inside Ella Gift pantalets.

Ovah deh side, ovah de side
She toss her pantalets ovah board
Ovah deh side, ovah deh side
She toss her pantalets ovah board.

DINAH

Dinah in the ring ah Dinah
Oh, ah oh Dinah
Dinah in the ring, ah Dinah
Oh, ah oh Dinah
Dinah say she loss her lover
Oh, ah oh Dinah

Dinah say she loss her lover
Oh, ah oh Dinah
Turn round gel and find yo lover
Oh, ah oh Dinah
Turn round gel and find yo lover
Oh, ah oh Dinah

This is the one you hug up last night
Oh, ah oh Dinah
This is the one yo hug up last night
Oh, ah oh Dinah

One Sunday morn, ah went the water gut
Ah meet two dog, ah stop he water gut
Ah tek two stone, ah bus he meemie gut
Jeh, heh, ho—he meemie gut, jeh, heh, ho

The Picnics

To the B.V.I. youth, a picnic is a fun time enjoyed by sea bathers on the beach or visitors to a national park or some other favorite spot where participants take their own refreshments.

To the older person, the term "picnic" conjures up the "gala" organized by persons such as Dan Farrington, Luther Scatliffe, Sammy Rhymer and others as part of the August festivities. In the good old days there was one August holiday—August Monday. After that, the rest of the week was filled out with picnics at Brewers Bay, Cane Garden Bay, Fahie Hill, Soldier's Hill, «The Station" (Agricultural Station) to which the public was invited by means of local posters written in pen and ink. These posters said:

"STOP! LOOK! READ!
COME ONE, COME ALL
THERE WILL BE A GRAND PICNIC AT . . . . (PLACE)
ON AUGUTST WEDNESDAY . . . .
FEE: GENTS 15 CENTS, LADIES 10 CENTS
CHILDREN 5 CENTS.

The main feature of the picnic was dancing to the music of a local band. It started around 10 a.m. and continued for the balance of the day. The fees mentioned above was the price of the dance, food, and drinks. Food usually included, stew goat, sheep, pork, peas soup, rice, potato, fried plantain.

The names of some famous picnic organizers are OLVA BREWLEY of FREE BOTTOM, WALLIE ROBINSON of MEYERS, SAMMY and ARNOLD RHYMER of BREWERS BAY, JOE PENN of SOLDIER'S HILL, DANIEL FARRINGTON of FAHIE HILL—perhaps the most popular picnic in its day—LUTHER SCATLIFFE of PASEA HALL, ERNEST PICKERING and SONS of BAUGHERS BAY, SAMMY FREEMAN of BAUGHERS BAY and SAM MALONE of BELLE VUE.

Musicians at these picnics would have been CYRIL BARONVILLE (and his bombodine) CARLIE PICKERING, LEO KENDALE, ERNEST BREWLEY, MERVIN PETERSON, RANDALL DAWSON.

150 YEARS AFTER!!! YOU CAN'T STOP US

MISS UNIVERSE PAGEANT IS AN EVERY YEAR OCCURRENCE

QUEEN DONNA FRETT MISS BVI 1983 IN "NATIONAL DRESS"
REPRESENTED BVI AT "MISS UNIVERSE" PAGEANT 1984

PICTURE OF DARWIN SCATLIFFE PLAYING HIS SAXOPHONE

THE GUN – DARWIN SCATLIFFE

1927 – 2005

Darwin "Gun" Scatliffe was born on July 28, 1927 to the late Hubert Scatliffe and Maude McIntosh in Tortola, British Virgin Islands. He was the second of two children. Darwin grew up in Huntum's Ghut and received his education at the Anglican School in Road Town.

His father introduced him to basket weaving at the early age of twelve, and his basket creations spanned some sixty-six (66) years. His creations included, but were not limited, to lamp shades, bottle holders, baby baskets and hampers. They were produced for Farmer's Week exhibitions, shops, tourists and locals alike. One of his faithful customers was Mr. Gregory Gunter of Sunny Caribbee.

His musical career started at the age of fourteen (14) when he purchased a saxophone in St. Thomas for the price of $50.00. His first song that he played with the Community Band was called "Everybody Sing Deh Calypso Man." Darwin later went on to form his own band "Gun and the Shots." He played at dances, picnics and weddings as well as serenaded during Christmas and New Year's. Darwin was multi-talented and played every instrument in his band.

In 1958, he married Julia Smith who preceded him in death. This union produced four children namely Dionisio (deceased), Denisia, Carmen, and Darwin Ricardo.

Darwin was an avid horse racing fan and owned two horses of his own namely, "Ever-ready" and "Miss Maude." They even nick named him "The Horse." The Last horse race that he attended was August Tuesday, 2005.

He was also a #1 fan and supporter of "Prime Time Band" where his son "Chicken" was the lead singer. We would say that Daddy was the public relations officer for the band because he seemed to know whenever or wherever the band would be playing.

Darwin was committed to his family and always made sure that they were provided for, especially his seven grandchildren with whom he developed a special bond with. He accepted Jesus Christ as Lord and Saviour of his life in September, 2005; his most important accomplishment.

Darwin lived a life that was dedicated to keeping culture alive in the BVI. The many awards of recognition that he earned throughout his life are testimonies to this. The British Virgin Islands has lost a stalwart native son who loved and was committed to his country, its people and rich heritage.

You have finished your course Darwin Scatliffe, now Rest in Peace.

LOUIE, LOUIE, LOOSE YO MULE

Louie, Louie, loose yo mule
Louie, Louie, loose yo mule
Louie, Louie, loose yo mule
Before he turd in front me do'

When Louie went to Brewers Bay
Riding on he father mule
The father turn an tell he Louie,
Louie loose yo mule

Louie, Louie, loose yo mule
Louie, Louie, loose yo mule
Louie, Louie, loose yo mule
Before he turd in front me do'

PIECE AH PUNKIN

Ah plant a piece ah punkin
Right before me do'
Ah plant a piece ah punkin
Right before me do'
Ah plant a piece ah punkin
Right before me do'
And the wind from Mary frock tail
Blow it right down.

To the songs we sang then, there was music played by some of the best musicians this Territory produced. These included musicians such as:

Albert Pickering
Carlie Pickering
Mervin Peterson
Randall Dawson
James "Nancy" Malone
Kenneth "Shorty" Fahie
Bregado Flax
Ernest Brewley
Cyril Baronville
Leo Kendall
Wendell Simon
Herman Abbott
Darwin "The Gun" Seatliff e
Allan O'Neal

It is told that in some areas villagers met in a cleared flat area on moonlight nights and the musicians would "strike up". a dance. Such dances would be polka, waltz, two and seven steps fifth figures and just plain ole "break away" dance--where everyone showed his particular style of dance interpretation. Young ladies took care not to get so carried away that they "wuk up" during the dance as this was not considered becoming. During final songs like "Now is the hour when we must say goodbye" caused guardians to look very closely at the closeness of the dancing couples. Our grandparents would be totally scandalized by today's dance where "wukking up" is the order of the day.

Eileene L. Parsons

MR. IRA SMITH, EXCELLENT TENOR VOICE THAT LED THE METHODIST CHOIR IN ANEGADA FOR MANY YEARS

"I walked a mile with Sorrow
And ne'er a word said she
But, oh, things I learned from her
When Sorrow walked with me.

(Along the Road—Robert Browning Hamilton)

IN

OUR

SORROW

In Our Sorrow

The future generation will probably not know what a 'wake' is, because this aspect of our culture is rapidly disappearing. In days gone by, the 'wake' was an important means of comfort and support for the bereaved family.

Relatives and friends gathered from far and near to the home of the bereaved where they sang hymns, offered prayers, and drank coffee and 'booze' until dawn. This helped to keep a family awake and to protect the corpse from being attacked by dogs if left alone. There was no mortuary then, and the corpse had to be kept at home. The house was kept open to allow the air to pass through at all times, and retard the process of decomposition during the 24 hour period between death and burial.

Today, death is announced by radio. There was no radio station in those days and the young reader will no doubt wonder how the word got around in times past. Well, in the country areas, someone with a loud voice stood on a hill and called as loudly as he could to the out-lying and adjacent villages, e.g. "On Brewers Bay" or "Oh Huntums Ghut" "Meyers", etc. When someone responded, the caller announced "Thomas John James dead". After that, the news spread by word of mouth from one to another. If the family of the deceased owned a horse or was able to get one from a neighbour a rider would be sent from village to village—not stopping—but announcing as he rode through—"Mamselle Ben dead" or Mamselle Ben gone".

Relatives and friends showed support in other ways. They dug the grave and built the coffin, free of charge. The gown for the female corpse was also made free of charge by a local seamstress. The family, on their part provided food and drinks for the workers. Much of this food—depending on the family's circumstances—was at times contributed by other family members and friends.

The body was buried in the family burial ground a sacred corner of the family land. The bereaved family showed their respect as well as their sorrow by wearing mourning for long periods of time, according to the closeness of the kinship between them and the deceased. For a husband or parent, for example mourning would continue for a year or more, but the period of mourning would be reduced as the relation became more distant. Mourning clothes would be black and the intensity of colour would be reduced as time passed or if the wearer was of "tender age". This meant black giving way to gray or black and white. There were some women who mourned the loss of husbands and sons or fathers for years on end just wearing a lesser shade of mourning as time passed.

Some of the well-known coffin makers were:

Randall Dawson
David Freeman
Evan Evans
Edwy Flax
Alexander O'Neal
Otto O'Neal
Alfred Vanterpool
Osmond and William Roach
Mikey Scatliff
Alfred Malone
Randolph Dawson

In the East End area the men who built the boats were the ones who were called upon to construct coffins at the time of death.

Some of the well-known grave diggers who helped out at the time of death were:

Owen Williams "Ruffinella"
Willie Niles
Owen Dawson
Larry McKelly
Edward Walters
Clarence Varlack
Irvin O'Neal

Eileene L. Parsons

Page from the Bulletin with

Althea Harrigan (Norwell Harrigan's mother)
Bertha Brodie (Beef Island Dentist from Belgium)
A.O. Norman (Writer and Captain)

The Hurricane of 1924 (August 28th)

In the early 1920's the British Virgin Islands were cut off from the outer world as there were no radios or telegraph offices on the islands. News traveled by letter and by word of mouth. These two methods of communication are entirely unsuitable for news of an approaching hurricane to get to the inhabitants of our islands. The question now arises: how did our parents and grandparents know when a hurricane was on its way?

The old folks looked at the sky and noted the black clouds and numerous weather birds (frigate birds) flying overhead. These, they said, were sure signs that bad weather was approaching. In Road Town, there was at least one barometer from which one was able to know when there was a low pressure area around. This again was a sure sign that bad weather was approaching.

The morning of August 28th was bright and people went about their work as usual. Before twelve, it started raining lightly but by one o'clock the rain had increased and so had the wind. Frigate birds were to be seen in great numbers and this was a sure sign that some foul weather was afoot. The winds increased, the clouds scurried across the darkening sky; thunder, lightning, rain and wind created the background for the approaching drama. Of course on a day like this, night will set in earlier and therefore people who feared that their homes are not safe, will move early to where (they hope) will be a safe storm shelter.

My grandfather, John Charles, decided to move his family from Old Yard to Parsons. They started out around five in the afternoon leaving everything behind, as he was skeptical about a hurricane approaching. He intended to return to the house, (after depositing his family); but when they finally got to Parsons, it was impossible for him to return on account of high winds and rain.

On arriving at Mr. John Thomas's house the family found many people already there. Indeed the house was full to overflowing. The children were soon put to bed; but, of course they did not sleep. As the winds increased, the house swayed from side to side and Mr. Thomas was heard to say "Hold, on old lady, hold on".

Suddenly, there was a lull, but luckily it did not last long enough to allow anyone to leave the house.

The winds did not take very long to be just as fierce as before and I am sure, many did not think they would live to see the morning. Next door, a house fell and the noise was heard above the shrieking of the winds and the crashing of the thunder.

About four o'clock next morning everything was quiet. The Charles' family, at break of day, picked their way home. On arrival the bare ground met them. The house was gone. Pieces found in a pond close by, and clothes and other belongings found half a mile away. This family was lucky to be alive and thanks must go to the nagging wife, who kept insisting that a move be made, before it was too late.

From Sea Cows Bay we move to Road Town for this account. By 4 p.m. the people at the Agricultural Station sounded a fog horn to warn the inhabitants that a hurricane was on its way. The people quickly got carpenters and other able men to secure their houses and boats as best they could.

At this time, the north-wind had raised waves which battered the coast from Hog's Point to Wickhams Cay. The intensity of the wind increased to a velocity estimated at 150-170 m.p.h. (This was enough force for a leaf to break a window). The waves rose to a height of 4 feet in Road Harbour. Houses were dislodged from their foundations and were tossed as far as 50 yards from their original positions. The wind blew down Government House and it carried the roof of the Fonseca's house in Road Town to the top of Joe's Hill.

Boats were destroyed in much the same way as the houses. Boats at Cleaning Hole were affected after the lull at midnight, when the wind changed direction and veered to the South and South-East. The boats were tossed into MacNamara and one schooner landed on the present site of the Government House tennis court.

When the inhabitants were able to open their windows, they gazed on a scene of thorough devastation. Dead fish and birds, most of which were pelicans, added to the overwhelming display of debris which clogged the narow streets. Plants and trees were destroyed. According to my father, J.R. O'Neal, there was not a leaf on Tortola to save your life.

In the West End area conditions were just as bad as in the two areas mentioned above. By early evening the wind became as strong as a giant, and the raindrops were so big and hit so hard that they seemed capable of chopping anything that was living. However, that was not the worst of it, for about twelve o'clock it had gotten so bad, that one might have sworn that the time for the Lord's return had come. That was by no means the last of the hurricane.

Even more interesting is the way the people tried to evade being harmed by the hurricane. The wind had blown down several houses and the people took to the hills to join the wild goats in search of shelter. They sought refuge under boulders, large trees and even under century plants (Coveous). The thing that conveyed their feeling of destruction to many minds was seeing a new house filled with cotton, catching afire and burning to ashes, though there was enough rain to flood the whole island falling on it. Naturally this was due to the lightning.

One thing of special notice was the mini-tidal wave. It went for as much as about two hundred yards in-land, though not up the hill. Fresh Water Pond Village claimed to have caught as many fishes in that pond as a fisherman with fifteen years' experience would have caught in his life time.

These three areas give us an idea of the seriousness of the 1924 hurricane. The old folk claimed that this hurricane was particularly bad, because it occurred on the night of the full moon and this belief is strong throughout the islands. The aftermath saw 25 people dead and countless injured Most of the dead were from Baugher's Bay where one family was totally wiped out except for one child. The hospital was torn down and patients were sent to St. Thomas. Within a week aid had come from central government in Antigua and from St. Thomas.

Barbara O'Neal, Dourell Vanterpool and Prudence Barry

(STRAIGHT FROM US, VOL. 1, #2 BY BVI HIGH SCHOOL

1867 - Fishlook book

1916 - Times article Elton George

1924 - Detailed account by the Commissioner serving at that time

1959 - Donna 1984 - Klaus

1989 - Hugo

1995 - Louis, Marilyn

1997 - Bertha
1999 - Lenny

Told by Jr. O'Neal, Leonell Donovan, (Survivor and Benjamin Romney)

WE WILL REMEMBER THEM.

Readers will agree that we have had a successful and very happy birthday number and it is unfortunate that it must end in a sombre tone. The brighter the sunlight - the deeper the shadows. It is with deepest regret that I have to record the passing of four well known Virgin Islanders.

On Sunday, March 8th, The Cottage Hospital saw the passing of our old friend Mrs. Bertha Brodie of Beef Island, at the age of 76 years. She had been ailing for the past six months, and the operation performed in Puerto Rico last September, of which high hopes were built for the restoration of her health, proved unsucessful. The quiet funeral, conducted by Rev. Davison, took place at Beef Island on Monday 9th. Mrs Brodie was Belgian and married a Scotchman who bought Beef Island for her in 1898. She actually came to settle here after the Great War and during that time spent only two holidays in England. She it was who taught the girls of the Virgin Islands to make the lace mats which have brought in many hundreds of dollars to the Territory.

On Sunday, March 15th at St Thomas Mrs. Althea Harrigan, wife of Mr. Alan Harrigan, passed away suddenly at the age of 53 years. She was for years an active social worker, a Sunday School teacher and Class Leader in our Methodist Church. In late years ill health compelled her to retire from those activities. The sad news of her death was brought to Road Town by special Motor boat the following Monday morning and Mr. and Mrs. Norwell Harrigan (her eldest son), other relatives and the minister left immediately for the funeral.

On Sunday, March 22nd, Mrs. Martha Damo died at her home in Jost van Dykes at the age of 75 years. For many years Mrs. Damo served the little community as local midwife and was most attentive in helping the doctor on his visits to the district.

On Monday, 23rd March, Captain Alpheus Osario Norman, aged 52 years, was killed at St Thomas when a steam shovel he was repairing collapsed, crushing him. The remains were brought home to Road Town the same evening by the Lady Kate for burial. The funeral took place at the Road Town Methodist cemetery next morning, the service being conducted by Reverend Davison. Captain Norman was a great student and was especially interested in West Indian history. He was an Antiguan by birth, and like the rest of them, was an intrepid sailor. He had a fund of interesting tales to tell of his many voyages and loved telling them.

The Virgin Islands have been the richer for the lives of these people. Our deep sympathy goes out to all relatives in their bereavement.

GOLDEN AGENDA PREPARED BY

TAMARA DAVIES - SEPTEMBER 1999

6# KRAFT

Virgin Islands Studies Committee Meeting

September 29, 1999

Agenda

1. Prayer and Welcome J.N.W.
2. President's remarks
2. Introduction of members
3. Individual presentations
   - Tamara Davies - Desktop Publishing
   - Rhonda Hodge - Projects
   - Carol Arneborg - Architecture/ Archaeology Research
   - Mitch Kent - Research
4. Wrap-up presentation J.N.W.
   - a. Present developments
   - b. The future - it looks bright
5. Final reactions
6. Adjournment

7-20